ANNE'S YOUTH

ANNE'S YOUTH

Frances Gladstone

Schocken Books　　New York

First published by Schocken Books 1984
10 9 8 7 6 5 4 3 2 1   84 85 86 87
Copyright © 1984 by Frances Gladstone

Library of Congress Cataloging in Publication Data
Gladstone, Frances.
Anne's youth.
I. Title.
PS3557.L2917A8   1984   813'.54   83–40459

Manufactured in the United States of America
Design by Cynthia Basil
ISBN 0–8052–3890–5

ANNE'S YOUTH

1

In the beginning the four of us, with my little sister who was born a year after me, lived in a grey housing project for poor families in New York City. The projects were like cars; each was identical, but you recognized your own anyway. Each apartment building had a circular, cement entrance with a red metal door, over which a bulb shined protectively all night, in a black metal cage. For some reason, I associated the grey, mechanical entrance with my father; perhaps because I always met him there when he came home from work in the evening. In front of each building was an oblong courtyard with benches, and trees, and barbed-wire fences. Everything was fenced in to protect us from the omni-present threat of thieves and marauding children. At night, a slight, barred light came through the metallic grille on the stoop.

The poor live on the stoops and in the hallways. (The middle-class goes inside to fight.) So one day as I was waiting for my father to come home, I sat on the metal steps in the hallway in front of our door, and an emaciated hag with long, painted orange fingernails and bleached hair like a scouring pad, came flying through the corridor. She was wearing an orange-pink housecoat with a lumpy cloth design, in imitation of the movie stars, which opened to reveal skinny, undernourished legs. After her ran her husband, who had just come home from work drunk. Then they both disappeared, the door banged shut, and bleating, hysterical noises came through for a long time, and then there was silence. Soon the children began to scream and hit one another, and I knew everything was all right; by the time it filtered to them, everything dangerous was over.

I knew their children would never be normal: they told jokes I didn't understand, they played with knives, and there was an unstrung nervousness about the whole family.

In those days I was placid, with two thick, brown braids and crossed blue eyes under pink, horn-rimmed glasses, and a full healthy stomach that always went a little bit ahead of me. Then my father's face had the handsome, unifying glow which health and purpose added to naturally harmonious features. But even in the early days, as I sat on our steps, I decided that reality had two sides, like a blanket: one was vicious and destructive and the other far away from our halls, in a realm of substance and beauty I had never seen, but in which I believed.

As I saw my neighbors murdering one another's souls, I already had an idea of a soul, or an internal something, which was distinct from what happened around you, I decided to be kind and good. I didn't ask myself to what I would be kind and good, but I thought that was my only defense against what I saw in our hallways and streets. The more deprivation I saw, the kinder I became; but a gap developed between the two extremes which took the form of constant loneliness. There was a cycle. Villany, the resolution to be kind, and loneliness. That, in turn, was only appeased by my father, who came home from his factory, and put me on his shoulders, laughing and saying that I weighed too much for one tired man. But he made me feel lonely in still another, deeper way that I have never understood.

So I invented this story.

Once upon a time there was a little man who traveled all over the world with a sack of memories on his back. He resembled the sandman in "Hansel and Gretel," which my mother played for us at night on the piano. Whenever he came to a new place, he put down his sack, and took out a memory or two to keep himself company. In this way he always had what he needed,

2

and everything was fine. But one day he lost his principal memory: the one which had given him the most comfort.

He looked everywhere, but apparently the memory had disappeared and would not come back. The old man couldn't remember what to do, and so he stopped, like a clock.

He spent all his time poking the earth, and sniffing, until he even forgot what he was looking for. He just went around in a perpetual circle, poking and sniffing from habit.

This might have gone on indefinitely, except one day someone took pity on him and slipped the memory of death into his sack. When he pulled this black envelope, like ashes, from his potato-cloth bag, the old man was glad, and thought it superior to all the others, since it put an end to them. And so he died, holding his sack.

My father's expression was like a poor, lost dog that has been neglected and badly treated, and so gotten into the habit of grumbling and not expecting much. Whenever I see that particular look, I know so-and-so comes from a poor family. It seems to say, "Look, sir, here we are and one of us is going to come out worse, so let's be plain, and get the unpleasant business over with. It's a dog-eat-dog world, and even if you're here today, you might be in the poorhouse tomorrow." According to my father, most of humanity was on the way to the poorhouse, or the graveyard. When one day I asked him where this mythological place was, he said, happily, "Schnukelpuss, a fool can ask more questions than a wise man can answer." Having given up on the world at an early age, he felt that his family was the only good left, and so he worked continuously, without thinking of anything else. He had the philosophy of the poor, who believe that life is work, and the rest up to women. "What happens inside the house is the woman's business," he often said.

There was another side to this face, which later became habitually distorted with malevolence and self-hatred. This other side appeared in the evening, when my father came home tired but energetic, after working eight hours in a factory.

As soon as dinner was over, and my mother had stuffed us all with huge portions of meat, and healthy vegetables, and pota-

3

toes (Jews eat as if someone were going to snatch their food away at any moment, and so they have to arm themselves by eating amazing bulk with equal rapidity), my father would get up, loosen his belt from his slender waist, and roll back the table-cloth from the thin, faded, wood table on which we ate, saying, "Okay. Time for me to go back to work. Look, Cookie, go play in the living room, and you, too, Susan. A man needs some peace and quiet." Then he took out a metal box of screwdrivers, hammers, and tools of all sizes, and until midnight repaired the radios and televisions the neighbors brought. Business flourished since my father was honest, meaning he charged very little for the meticulous work involved, and most of the repairmen, "shysters," as he put it, who would replace good parts and then charge for them. "It don't pay to cheat, Cookie," my father often said. "Ya got to be honest. The others cheat, but it only gets them an ulcer, or they land in the nut-house. And, besides, you lose business. People find out. Me, I do honest work for honest pay." The truth was that he was afraid to overcharge or remove tubes because, although he was naturally intelligent, he lacked the imagination of a crook. He had the idea, well-rooted in his head, that pay should be equal to hourly labor. In return for his naive honesty, he was always exploited by someone more cunning, who turned my father's simple, clever discoveries into profit. In addition, he had a deep, childhood fear of tampering with authority . . . and authority had it that you got paid for what you did. So my father worked continuously, and disassembled and reassembled and poked with an infinity of tools into the machines that poured into our apartment from all sides, until, with his natural alertness, and by studying mathematics and such subjects at night, he trained himself to be an engineer. "Ya can't beat the system," he often said. "I'm a Jew and they know no one will hire me."

In the back of his mind was the idea that by improving himself, he would make a better salary, so we could move out of our apartment and buy a house. Owning a house was commensurate with providing for his family. His face was wonderfully full during those long hours, like the green, healthy spring when each element is busy with its own purpose and growth, questioning nothing about the meaning or direction of its existence.

4

With all his tools he bent over our flimsy wooden table for hours in a red check lumberjack shirt, striped with black and yellow bars, and grey workers pants, an old-fashioned, gold watch with a pink face on his thin wrist: his handsome cheeks had color, and he was at peace. At midnight he would stop, scoop whatever machine he was repairing into a pile together with its parts, and put it in a corner in some old newspaper. Then he would collect the tools, and put each back into the metal box, which he locked and put away for the night.

The picture of him working night after night to improve his family, bent over our table, has burned itself into my mind, like love, together with a feeling of incommensurate pain; pain that is incommensurate with what happened later.

When my sister and I were washed and in our pajamas, my father came in and sat on the edge of our bed and usually began a serenade of those ancient English songs which are never taught, but handed down, and appear when adults lapse into whatever-they-wish—in short, when no one is listening and they can wrap themselves in the most comfortable of all feelings: milky sentimentality. In a low growl that was devoid of music, since it missed the high and low notes and only showed a modification in energy where there should have been a shift in melody, in a voice without tune but full of resonance and good humor, my father sang to us of dying minstrels who clutched their harps, and elegant fish who gave birth to humans, of swooning ladies and sailors who were out of their minds. He sang about misshapen animals, or orphans, or woebegone creatures in general, laughing about those unmentionable activities that occupy ninety percent of human energy and thought and about which we never speak. In any case, whenever there was a homeless this, or an unhappy, unloved that, I felt he was singing, endlessly, tunelessly, about himself. There was a peculiar emphasis in his eyes and voice, which made me think so, together with laughter which reminded me of the pretty, lost dog.

He rarely spoke about himself; that was against the rules. In fact, introspection of any kind was a dangerous activity, and one likely to accelerate your progress to the bug-house. He assumed that life was hard, and the only thing to do was to

5

keep going. His memory took the form of buried nostalgia. If there had been a myth for my father, it would have been this: once upon a time there was a brave man who worked hard all his life and never looked back. But he perceived, as he got older, that he bent closer and closer to the ground, and his back hurt, and his fingers, with which he earned his living, grew thick and moved with difficulty. But he continued going, with the one proviso that he never look back. In this way, his wife died, his children left, and he was all alone. But still he never looked back. He was like a horse with blinders. Then one day curiosity got hold of him, and he couldn't control himself. He tried to keep going, but he couldn't manage it. Then he turned around, and looking into the past saw the hatred his wife had felt for the fifteen years they were married. One child was in a mental institution with hideous delusions, and his own mother dead of malnutrition. "Ghosts, corpses," he thought, "the rule was not to look back." But it was too late; he ripped off his blinders, his back gave in altogether, and shuddering in horror, he died.

But that is only a myth.

He usually seemed remote from his own troubles, as if they had happened to someone else to whom he happened to be attached. His manner said, "Yes, Cookie, that's how it is. It's a dog-eat-dog world. And don't let them kid you." According to his tacit, masculine code you never discussed feeling and so everything remained a matter of songs, and poorhouses, and graveyards. He seemed to expect very little except abuse, even in the beginning, for this other person to whom he was attached.

Sometimes I asked him to tell us the story of Bunsha Schweig. Although he was inwardly pleased, my father usually said, "You girls will put a man in an early grave. But all right, if you listen and don't interrupt." Then he told this story:

In a certain town, somewhere in Eastern Europe, Bunsha Schweig lived and never went very far to the left or right, or up or down, and generally minded his business. However, if something fell from a window onto his sparsely covered head, which is to say he was almost bald, or if a bird going south needed to express itself, Bunsha often happened to be underneath; or if

6

some housewives were cursing or yelling about their rotten fates, Bunsha often happened to be passing by and thought they were talking about him. However he never said anything, because after all, what was there to say? In the course of things Bunsha lost his job and became ill, and his friends accused him of having done things he did not know existed, and still he kept silent and went neither very far to the left or right, or up or down. Soon after this he got seriously ill, looked very miserable, and died; but right until the end he said nothing, he never complained because there was nothing, really, to say. Instead he went directly to heaven and stood as he usually did, trying to hide his head inside his shirt in front of the admittance gate. To the left stood the prosecuting angel, and to the right the defending angel, and further behind was the throne of the Lord Himself in a blaze of gold. Bunsha stood there trembling silently, wondering what the big ones would do with him.

The prosecuting angel fussed around as usual, and huffed himself into a lump as if he were going to make a speech, but then he changed his mind and said, admitting defeat, "Bunsha. All your life you were silent; now I, too, have nothing to say." Then the defending angel was very pleased because his job was done, and fluttering his wings like a fan, he opened the gate that led directly to the throne of God, but of course Bunsha was afraid to look.

"Bunsha," the Lord said, bending toward him, "all your life you never asked for anything. Now, if you could have anything, what would you want?"

"Anything?" he asked timidly, as if he suspected a trick, but then reminded himself that the Lord didn't do such things.

The Lord nodded.

"Anything," Bunsha repeated, "no one will be angry?"

The Lord nodded again, to indicate that no one would hurt Bunsha.

"Well, in that case, your majesty," Bunsha said, getting it wrong as usual, "if it isn't too much trouble, I would like a hot white roll with butter in the morning."

Then even the Lord was ashamed, and hung his head.

"Well girls, that's enough for tonight," my father would say, "I got to go back to work. It's a woman's story. Sleep tight."

7

I put together my father's life sideways, from little bits of this and that, since he would never discuss himself. Discussing oneself was an indulgence for the rich or crazy, in which category he placed artists, professors, psychiatrists, and overly-made-up women.

Apparently, no sooner was he born than his father, beholding his unwanted product, disappeared forever, leaving his young wife with the little baby. A bad situation became worse and his mother, who seems to have been meek and selfless by nature, in short, she possessed in a heap all those unsatisfied qualities we attribute to the madonna, tried unsuccessfully to support her child. When the Depression came, she abandoned the effort and reluctantly placed him in an orphanage to shield him from her own life.

I know only one fact about this place. "Well, Cookie," he once said. "They hit you on the hand with a ruler every morning for all the things they wouldn't catch during the day." Finally a family adopted him, and soon after, he went to work in a factory.

That was during the Depression, when there was no system of scholarships for the poor, such as we have now, or have had until recently. So when my father, because of his natural intelligence and mechanical aptitude, was accepted into a good technical university, he could not go.

I have only two concrete facts about my grandmother whom I never met. The first is a lost look, like an internal bleat, on my father's face whenever he spoke about her: it is a mixture of love and resentment for the fact that the one person responsible for him, abandoned him. It says, "See. There's no relief." At such moments, like a piece of the truth, the little lost dog appeared, extant and vulnerable, in spite of the powerful, adult man.

I sensed that my father associated love with abandonment, and following the rule that people do back to others what has been done to them. He later abandoned everything he loved . . . but that is my own opinion. As I listened to him, I realized that there was something special, irreplaceable about his mother and if you showed him a hundred women, each very much like her, it still would not do.

8

The second fact is a precious band of diamonds, made of little, alternating squares and hexagons, which my grandmother bought for my mother. It is an old-fashioned ring of the type that are no longer made, in which each perfect diamond is carefully set in platinum. My mother rarely wore it. "Why should I wear it when I do the dishes, and the diamonds can fall out, or to lose it. Yes. She didn't have any money. She was always starving, but she bought it before we were married." So the ring stayed wrapped in white cotton, in a white leather case with a clasp in our secretary drawer, and only emerged from there on special occasions.

How my grandmother must have pinched and saved to buy her daughter-in-law that ring and compensate, by a single act, for what she had been unable to do during her life. In any case, she bought the ring, they were married, and my grandmother died a year before I was born. A vulnerable look of pain, like a little bleat, escaped from my father from time-to-time as the only commemoration of the fact that she had ever existed.

My father hated, systematically, all those who were successful. "The rich," he would say, using a form of subway English which he deliberately kept, in spite of his intelligence, as a stubborn token that he identified with the poor and uneducated, "the rich don't stink no better." And paradoxically, he totally accepted the standards which had forced him into his life. "Ya got to work," he would say. "Those who live on welfare are not functioning members of society. Ya don't get something for nothing. And let me tell you a little fact, those others who give themselves fancy airs and think they're too good to work like everyone else, they're on the way to the bug-house. There's no alternative, no one ever gave me nothin' except a hard time, and the only things that are free are the poorhouse, or a beggar's grave. . . . Where are they? I'm not saying that ya got to be miserable all the time, but the only thing free is poverty. And let me tell you," he would add, narrowing his beautiful blue eyes which had unhealthy bits of white mucous at the corners, "when you're in the poorhouse, don't expect any help because there's only one place left and that won't keep you warm."

Then he often sang a low, tuneless song to emphasize his

9

point, laughing inwardly at something gross and unmention-able in existence. "Oh the worms will crawl in and the worms will crawl out. They'll crawl in your nose and come out of your mouth." He seemed to relish the picture of worms going back and forth as a comment on human aspiration.

But more often, the natural lucidity of his mind was replaced by an unattractive look, a mixture of suspicion and pain, like the poor, pretty lost dog who has been badly fed and beaten a lot, and so developed the habit of snarling.

2

My mother's face is like a porcelain doll which has little, out-lined features that might be pretty because of something frag-ile and coquettish in them. As it is, however, she looks out at the world with small, suspicious eyes and the conviction that something will go wrong or that someone is trying to hurt her. There is a cunning, hysterical gleam in her eyes that seems to say, "Watch out if you think you're going to pull anything over me, because I'm prepared for all your tricks, and besides, where I came from, we were all put away. Gassed. All of us, that is, who didn't escape." She is always about to cry. Even on those rare occasions when she laughs, you are not sure if she is not really crying but in reverse. Today she goes in and out of her low-income apartment, like the one where we all began, in a daily effort to combat the enemy, whom she has combined with the Marxist dialectic of thesis, antithesis, stasis, or depres-sion, struggle, new depression, and struggle. This enemy wants to keep her oppressed, poor, and ignorant. Most of the theory, as she makes her rounds between the knifings and murders that occur daily in her courtyard or under her window, has become struggle, and the resolution, or new position, has faded into a future that is pushed forward to the days when all the persecuted of this earth will be liberated. This enemy was originally a compound of Hitler and my father, but now he has swelled and taken over everything. "They are all exploiters," she says, referring knowingly to an indefinite "they," "and they

11

think they can shit on me because I'm a woman . . . but I'll show them. To struggle, Anne, to live, because let me tell you without struggle there's no life. That's what's important. Oh!" She always mispronounces my name.

She never developed beyond the age of thirteen, when she first began to flirt. My mother was born to sit in an ice-cream parlour, surrounded by courteous admirers with an adequate salary or else to cook mammoth, tasteless German meals. Instead she walked into a world war.

My mother's parents were arrested, and died in concentration camps soon after she left Germany in 1939; she was an orphan at eighteen.

People always justify their inner state with their philosophy. So, with a trapped, slate-like expression I have often seen on the faces of women who have lived a long time with a man they cannot bear, my mother struggles among the vitamins and counter-vitamins that line her kitchen, together with plastic containers of hormones and various amino acids. Each vitamin has an equal and opposite, in the form of another vitamin or secretion, and the trick is to discover and balance them all, and then match the entire, expensive collection to her body.

"Nobody can tell me what my body needs, Anne," she says, getting the vowel all wrong. "They," meaning the doctors, "are only out to schmooze you." *Schmooze* is her own word, meaning *to lie*. "I know my own system, and nobody else can tell me . . . the trouble is that I eat all the time and I'm losing weight so I'm afraid of cancer. If I die, well, my new diet is helping. My eyes don't close so much in the morning and the circulation is better. Come, have some powdered milk. It's soothing for the nerves, and not fattening. I have to watch the cholesterol and also the vitamin B-2. Did you know that vitamin B-2 controls the eyes and circulation? Yes, I found a new man, well, not exactly a doctor, but he is very good, very warm, who diagnosed me and discovered the problems. For years those other idiots . . . well . . . the important thing is not to give in, not to let them get you."

So she divides her hours into non-fattening portions of this and that, and every two years there is a new diet, more advanced than the last, which guarantees renewed vigor and mental alertness. "How do you know this one is better than the last?" I once asked, referring to a change from a two-year regime of liver and yogurt. She looked a little frightened, put her nose into the air, reflected, and then said, "I know my body's needs. No one can tell me. This one makes me feel better."

Her long, monotonous days are rounded by little pockets of reading, between which she sleeps on the couch in the living room among the clutter that has grown up around her, or else has diluted cups of powdered milk. She reads a paragraph or two about sociology, or women's rights, or the travail of so-and-so, then falls asleep and wakes up a quarter-of-an-hour later to try to remember what she has just read.

Art, for her, is the evocation of sympathy for the poor. If I suggest that it has other functions, to show the possibilities of thought or feeling, for example, in other words to describe what can be imagined as well as what is, she looks at me and it is clear that she is wondering how her own daughter can be so stupid. Then getting the vowel wrong again, and poking her nose into the air, which is always the sign that you are going to hear something you won't like—truth is something she alone knows, which the other does not want to hear—she says:

"I don't know why you turned out . . . ach, how can my child, to be so arrogant and bourgeois. Art is for the poor. That's what's moving . . . to show their suffering, their hardship. And you coming from a Marxist background . . . I don't know what I did wrong. I tried . . . how could I produce such a cold child, with no feeling for humanity." Then the nose comes down, the attack is over, and she begins to cry. Two things are intolerable: pain and your mother's tears. In any case, she says, "Well, let's have something to eat. I don't want to fight with you since you are my daughter, and I love my two girls more than anything else on earth. You are the most precious, ach . . ." Then more tears, during which time I have the recurrent feeling that my own flesh is in pain; in fact, I never watch my mother cry without at the same time experiencing a feeling of intense shame and self-loathing because we are both women.

When she closes the blinds in her apartment, she generally takes off all her clothes for the sake of her circulation and goes

13

back and forth among all the clutter in large underpants that predate World War II, and look like a remnant of labor. They are a greyish-white, and the shreds that have accumulated are gathered at the hips and held together on each side by a large safety pin. When she once came to the door to let me in dressed in nothing but those deteriorated underpants, I said, "Moo," which is a short, bovine form of Motte, "You haven't changed your underwear in ten years." She looked at me silently, with the cold, suspicious look she reserves for enemies. Then she said, "Well, no one can see, and where is my lover, anyway."

When I see her standing naked in the doorway, I have the same feeling that my own body is vulnerable and in pain and this has done me the most harm.

Her story began more than fifty years ago in Berlin. There her father's principal functions were to pick his nose, which in the process became visibly distended, and to have violent fits of jealousy with his wife, who was perfectly good and faithful but who had made the mistake of marrying a weak, ineffective man.

In the one picture of them my mother kept, my plump grandmother with her full, maternal bosom and thick, brown hair piled on her head like a hive, was seated next to my grandfather, a skinny man with a suspicious, withdrawn expression and a thatch of greying hair which was cut close at the sides so that he looked like a broom. The picture reminded me of the old-fashioned soap and perfume advertisements.

Apparently, the more he sensed his wife's quality and energy, the more crazed and unsure my grandfather became until the imbalance took the form of constant, unjustified fits of jealousy. From him a niche developed in my mother's mind, filled successively by Hitler and my father, of weak, frustrated men who abused their innocent wives.

They had a shoe store in a Jewish, bourgeois section of Berlin about which my mother said, with a look that implied, "Sheis, I will tell you the truth, with no schmoozing." Here it is a compound, as far as I can tell, of sugar and something German meaning to lie. In any case, she said, "Well, we had a store but they never sold anything. Whenever a customer came in they started fighting and got the wrong size, or else they didn't

14

have the right color, or the customer had a corn, so by the time they had agreed what to show and found it, the customer got fed up and left. Then they fought again about what they did wrong, or what size foot the customer had, or whether it was straight or crooked and why they didn't make a sale. When the war started, nobody came in and they just argued. My father was, well, what can you say, a schlemazl, who only picked his nose which got larger and larger. Sometimes he even used a toothpick to help so the hairs hung out. And my mother?" Here something approving and warm lighted my mother's face which I almost never saw happy. "She was a martyr, and perfectly loyal . . . only she had no life with that idiot. At the last minute, when it was impossible to get out, no one got their papers any more, and people disappeared, well, I went to the passport office. I looked on a table heaped with thousands of papers and by luck I found mine. Then I left Germany and soon after, I learned that they both had been killed in concentration camps. Gassed." When she speaks about them, her face has the look of a prisoner who has been put in jail for something he neither did, nor did not do, but which has happened anyway and has crawled into his mind in the place where life and the capacity for joy used to be. "You see," she added, "I think my mother stayed so that I could leave. Ach." Here she often took a toothpick and poked at the spaces between her unhealthy teeth as she cried. At such moments I had the feeling that the snow that holds creation up was somehow giving way.

At night when I was a little girl, my mother told me about the concentration camps in minute detail. That was when the feeling that my own flesh was vulnerable and in pain began, and I came to the conclusion that parents try to kill their children. As a result of these nocturnal tales, I had the following, repetitive nightmare.

I was in a long, dark chamber. Far away at the other end Hitler sat on a throne, waiting for me to walk down the hallway until I arrived at his seat. I was terrified because I knew I would be destroyed by the faceless, bodyless presence in the chair. But for some reason, fate was pushing me down the corridor. On either side of me naked, emaciated skeletons were taking gas showers and washing their corpses in the dark. They knew they would soon be turned into soap and their silent, fleshless bodies w̲ ̲e totally caught and unaware of me. Then with slow steps I walked, or was rather pushed by the same, relentless force along a red carpet toward the throne. The dream always stopped before I got to the other end of the hall where Hitler sat, but I knew I would be destroyed. When I awoke, I decided that the worst possible thing was to die alone and unseen, in the dark.

Now, thirty years later, there is an implacable internal enemy who creeps into my mother's circulation, drives her to nourish herself with non-fattening bits of this and that and worse, gives her dizzy spells with the latent threat of cancer. At times, when she overcomes these forces that lurk everywhere, she rises from her usual state in which her thin mouth looks like a rotting dash. Then removing her tortoise-shell glasses which are attached to her nose by a red string she has crocheted, and touching a packet of salt or sugar, or pepper or catsup which she has taken from a nearby restaurant to keep from being totally exploited by the owner, she says, with a frenzied, triumphant glitter in her unhappy, shrewd eyes, "Never forget that I love you two girls more than anything else. I'm very proud of you . . . you're the best thing I've done. The rest is, well, that's life. What can I do if I married a beast, an insensitive . . ."

Her dominion, however, is vast. It includes all the elements, drinkable and otherwise, in her apartment and most important, a relentless battle to understand which is permanently tangled with the Marxist dialectic. "Yes, Anne," she says, not realizing that she has dropped everything but the antithesis part of the theory, "The important thing is to develop one's potential. That's what life is. To struggle. To feel. Not to be dead inside, because let me tell you, there are many who make good money and are dead. To understand, Anne, to understand. Not to give in. To learn by one's mistakes. To go forward. That's what life is. Oh! It's so bwuteeful."

3

We visited Sara and Michael every Sunday for ten years in our dark, green Plymouth. It was the old fashioned, indestructible type of car that is no longer made and which, because of the grill under its nose, or hood, reminded me of my father's moustache: it had the same melancholy, sturdy, slightly foxy expression as he.

As we drove, I asked questions continuously. Were we half-way there, a quarter-of-the-way, was it still half-an-hour and so on, until I heard the invariable, "Cookie, a fool can ask more questions than a wise man can answer." So I waited a minute and then began again or else put my head on my father's knee and went to sleep, from all of which I developed a keen sense of security associated with our car, which probably had to do with the constant gas leak as well. My father's proverbs had one peculiarity; he derived his authority from I don't know where and it often seemed to me that the fool and the wise man were rather interchangeable, or at least liable to a lot of hopping around as far as who was who went. So whenever someone refers to an omnipotent authority, I immediately smell a gas leak. I always have. Even in the early days when my father loved to be pestered by my questions and took delight in the lively intelligence they showed, even then a disturbance was being created. Often in the middle of the night, during that portion of sleep which collects the day's impressions, I had the following nightmare from which I awoke terrified.

I was in my father's Plymouth. I was seated at the steering wheel, and I had to drive, although I didn't know how. I knew the car was headed over a cliff, and that I would be destroyed when the motor started. A powerful, faceless force pushed down the gas pedal, there were no hands on the steering wheel, the car started and I woke up before it went out over the cliff.

This dream was like the nightmare about Hitler . . . and so, later, I came to agree with Plato who says that the best thing in life is a long, dreamless sleep.

In any case, we arrived in front of Sara and Michael's white brick house, in a block of identical, attached houses like teeth. Soon Aunt Sara came out, wiping her immaculate fingers, which I imagined had been drained of their sap but managed to stay alive anyway, on her apron, while Michael sat inside at the kitchen table copying his eternal postcards onto oil canvases, more with his nose than his paintbrushes because his eyes were so bad.

As soon as I saw Sara's martyred, passive face I took out my other world and held firmly onto it as she led us into the kitchen. Sara was one of those people who cleaned up dirt before it appeared, and was always destroying imaginary bits of fluff and grease with a deft movement of her fingers, or else checking to see that her thin, equally sapless hair had preserved the contours of the rollers she had on the night before. She was neither old nor young but had always been her present age, like a flower that had never bloomed and had gone directly into a state of dry preservation. In a word, her expression seemed to say, "What's wrong? Don't you realize you're like everyone else and things could always get worse?"

She was of medium height and tucked her hair into a net as a remnant of the eight hours a day she spent in a noodle factory where she had worked for ten years, ever since arriving in America. Michael had apparently saved her life by helping her escape and for that reason, she never complained or disagreed and usually contented herself with, "Don't shout, Michael. It's bad for your nerves." She measured everything in silent, frugal portions as if life, too, like her table which was set with white, porcelain dishes with a litle pink rose pattern, had been deprived of its fat.

I imagined that Aunt Sara flew from her mother's womb with exactly the same expression on her face, as if she were about to smell something bad, until one day I saw a seductive woman with bare shoulders draped in dark, thick velvet in a fuzzy picture of the old-fashioned type. A coquettish curl hung over large, dark eyes and I asked Michael who the pretty lady was. "Dat vas die Sara; that was Sara," he replied, in a tone of pride in ownership. As I went back to the kitchen Sara looked at me and said in a high monotone which rose into a question at the end, although she was not asking one (in short, in that infantile tone of voice adults, who don't realize that children understand things, use), she said for the hundredth time, "Du bist ein shöne, grosse, süsse, kleine, madel, Anne. You are a pretty, big, sweet, small, little girl, Anne." Then as her voice rose to an absurdly high level where the childishness clashed against the German intonations so that I really wanted to escape, she took me into the broom closet and put a few dollars into my hand, reminding me not to tell Uncle Michael. Waste was the enemy to Michael as dirt was to Sara, and she functioned as a sort of aide-de-camp by eliminating both before they occurred. While we were still in the broom closet, as I put the money into a pocket in my pants, she asked me, "If a train was coming, who would you pull off the tracks? Your mother or your father?" I just looked at her, I didn't answer. I thought she was exactly like my mother, but I sensed, too, that she was doing whatever it was because she had no children of her own.

By compensation, Michael was a jangling mass of complaints and had an uncontrollable left eye which flew around in his head by a kind of sympathetic jolting whenever he was angry, which was often. It was hard to trace the chronology of all his aches, but as far as I could tell, he was either wounded or shell shocked in World War I and had somehow been limping along with one eye ever since. I always had the feeling that it was shock, more than a physical wound, which had started the horrible shaking that often made him resemble children's puppets in which all the parts are attached by coiled springs. If you touch them anywhere, the entire doll starts shaking, and each part goes off in its own direction. In spite of this, he still managed to work as a tailor by tracing the seams piecemeal, as much with his nose as his eyes.

Michael, generally, did not like anything, but he had two passionate, fastidious hobbies: by voluntary agreement everyone humored him about them, since in that way, there was peace. The first was a rosegarden from which he triumphantly produced healthy red and pink roses which he put into a white porcelain vase with little bumps on the kitchen table.

The second, in which I imagined that he made a private, stationary tour of the world, consisted of copying postcards or photographs of Alpine slopes or still lives, onto thick canvases with oil colors from a wood palette. He would put down his brush, squint, take off his glasses and then peer mainly with his nostrils to see if his imitation matched the original. He never attempted anything that was not already there in front of him. Perhaps he felt that the effort to collect houses, and mountains, and fruit, and so on, into a whole would be a strain on his imaginative faculty. In any case, these pictures of his were always framed and hung around the house which, for this reason, was decorated by mountains and Swiss hillsides in which each element stayed inside the myopic, black oil color outline with which he had traced its boundary. Perhaps it was because he was so near-sighted, and because he was always imitating something already there, that everything had a thick, stationary outline.

Like many nervous, sickly people, Michael thought that most of the world was "verruckt, crazy," or else, "meshugganah," which was a less dangerous, more affectionate form of the same obstruction to his diminutive universe. It never occurred to him that he himself might be wrong, or that there were ways to test and examine what you believe and so a ridiculous, masculine tyranny over the dishes and furniture, and most of all, over Sara developed. If he had thought about it, he would probably have liked Sara in the same way he liked his chicken soup, neat bed, and clean floor.

Our meals were always the same. Sara laid the table, wiping up imaginary dirt with her fingers, and then we had home-made chicken soup with noodles that came in little packages from her factory. How I hated that soup. It was like a prisoner's ration and to this day I cannot eat it. Then followed

20

fleish mit kartoffel, meat and potatoes, in meager portions, so as to avoid waste.

When we were all beginning to feel full, by a kind of mutual contrariness a terrible, loud row usually broke out between Michael and my mother about the rights of Negroes, or women, or the vast numbers of unskilled workers that had emigrated to America.

These battles always had the same conclusion. Michael's eye rattled around horribly in his head, he shook all over and scraped back his chair as if preparing to leave the table, while Sara told him to be careful and not upset his nerves or he'd have to go to the doctor. My mother, meanwhile, was expressing a more humane opinion but knocking against a hopeless tincan, she had never learned that unleashing the truth can be like throwing seeds on barren, depleted earth where they will only bounce back fruitlessly. In any case, she sat in her chair looking at some imaginary sympathizer out the window, or under the table, with the conviction in her face that all men were tyrants and that she alone understood the truth, and further, that she was hopelessly misunderstood.

Michael was one of those people who, although they have a very meager place in society themselves, clutch stubbornly at every prejudice that is contrary to their own common sense so long as it maintains others below them. By the same line of reasoning, he often extolled such and such a business man because he had crystal glassware, or because his wife wore a fine fur coat. He did all this unawares. He only said what he believed. However, what he believed maintained his own social position exactly where it was. My father said little, remarking in his increasingly withdrawn way that all this screaming would make Michael ill, and as for my mother, her ideas would land her in the bug-house where she was already headed. He usually added, "By the way, there are plenty there waiting for you. You'll have good company." There was a tacit bond between Michael and my father, since both classed my mother among the "ver-ruckt" and both thought that women should remain silent when there was company. My sister looked very lost at these times, and I thought about my other world, beyond the reach of chicken soup and nerves.

21

Soon cheesecake and coffee came and my mother inquired about Michael's paintings and roses, so things were quiet. If anyone had asked why we went through the same procedure each Sunday, my mother would have said, "We are relatives. Sara is my mother's sister, the one who was killed at Dachau, from the other side," as if that made everything clear.

When it was almost dark, and I was sleeping in their bedroom, and Sara had finished the dishes and taken off her rubber gloves, I heard, "Wake up schnukelpuss. Get up sleepyhead. Time to go home. I want to avoid the Sunday drivers." My father had one category for women drivers and another for Sunday drivers, and occasionally the two overlapped. As I lifted up the white cotton bedspread with its old-fashioned pattern of diagonal lumps, I noticed a bottle of 4711 Cologne and a paperback copy of *Nana* by Zola, on top of the bedstead. I wondered what interest a plump, naked woman wrapped in white gauze could have for anyone, and especially for Michael, but ten years later when I went to live downstairs, next to their boiler room, the same bottle of cologne and *Nana* were in exactly the same position over the bed. The difference between Michael and my mother, who both showed symptoms of war, was that my mother thought people were actively trying to take something from her, whereas Michael felt he would be safe if he somehow held on to what he had already accumulated.

I remember Sara standing on her stoop with her hands folded over her apron at sunset; with hands over a stomach that had never swelled with children or much pleasure either. As she said good-bye, she had the same crying thing in her voice that my mother had, which I have never heard without at the same time feeling involuntary self disgust. As she chirped like a skinny bird in her high, monotone voice, in which I heard fingers eternally doing the dishes, "Cum gut nach hause: get safely home." I felt that she was pushing us relentlessly with the same dim destruction that had gripped her into the inevitable something that waited for us in our house.

4

Before I could read, my other world lacked boundaries and definition. It only existed hypothetically, like vague, dreamy luggage whose weight bothers you from time to time, as if to say, "See. Here I am. And you thought you were content with your gorilla-like braids and crossed eyes. No such thing . . . and don't delude yourself into thinking you're like the others. There's no easy escape for you. You are definitely stuck with yourself, with your big stomach and your own way of seeing things, so you better find an ally."

1

In the first grade they thought I was retarded because I could not read. In fact, they tried to teach us in gulps, a whole word at a time, and since I could never get beyond the first letter, I could never manage the whole gulp.

One day our broom-stick teacher, who treated the whole class as if we were her husband, was particularly frustrated and cross. Partly because the neighborhood was changing from white to black so that she was forced to teach Negro children in order not to lose her job, and partly because she was in the mood to punish someone, she called two Negro twins to the front of the class and made them take down their pants. Then she got out a ruler. Those were the days when corporal punishment had just been declared illegal in the elementary schools, so teachers still did what they wanted.

In a gesture of shame, the two boys put their hands over their underpants and looked at the class to see if there was any sympathy for them. There wasn't, from which I learned again that people, even little ones, do back what has been done to them. The two boys grinned and cried at the same time when the teacher hit them. The others looked and enjoyed the sight, although the boys hadn't done anything that the rest of us did not do all the time.

I looked down at my books which I could not understand, and my sturdy leather briefcase, and I was ashamed. I thought the others shouldn't have looked. What was being done was cruel, and unjust, and the result of disgusting prejudice, but I also envied them for looking and I wanted to be like them. In the same instant, as the class glared and the boys stood covering themselves and smiling, a little voice whispered to me, "The twins are your brothers. This is shameful and this is the way it will always be."

The hitting with a ruler formed a boundary. I knew I would never look and I would never be like the others. In addition, I said nothing to the two boys because their sympathy was with the pack and they accepted that someone had to be sacrificed from time to time. A persistent inner voice repeated, "It's shameful and you are alone."

2

One day my mother took me home and by dint of ear-cracking screams, the English alphabet rang out through the house in mighty Germanic tones. Then the English and the German "r" and other transatlantic vowels hissed and fought to smash one another. When, as I said, she had screamed and pulled my braids and generally identified learning with torture as our collateral yelling covered the kitchen table, and the Knabe piano in the living room, I finally began to read after two weeks, by sounding out each word syllabically until it matched something I already knew. That is how you learn: by placing something new on top of something old.

Two weeks later I went to the head of my class, where I stayed.

3

In the third grade I fell properly in love.

Mrs. Purvis always dressed in black, with a little black hat and a veil under which her eyes, which were a greenish-purple, gleamed in their particularly calm, mysterious way. They upset me no end, those eyes, until I decided they were like orchids; then they bothered me less. So it is that when you name a thing, or fix a description to it, you feel more secure. Her dark, olive skin was always lightened by a little sweet-smelling white powder, and from between her neck and heavy bosom, there came a marvelous smell of thick, oriental perfume.

She was from Persia. Although I knew there was another part of the world where women wore perfume that lasted all night, and told stories for a thousand days to one man, who was for some reason surrounded by women as numerous as bees, while all sorts of beheadings and other atrocities were committed at his command, and although I had seen detailed gold and purple miniatures of all these doings, I had never met such a person and I was convinced she had a secret. As is often true of people who are heavy, she walked with a slight hump from the effort to keep her chest erect, which in turn created a rolling motion of her shoulders and hips. She would have looked strained and taxed by her own weight if her whole body had not been held together so gracefully, as if by some internal honey.

I never asked myself if she was intelligent, or if I learned anything from her, or why she seemed to accept our dingy, brick school building and her rather poor, indifferent clothing; instead I swam in a kind of well-being whose purpose was to please her and be loved in return.

I would have flown down the fire escape, or handed in heroic bits of homework, or memorized facts till I was blue if it would have made her happy. But that was the odd thing. She never asked me to do anything and, in fact, let me chatter incessantly, as if she understood that I was lonely and bored.

Only occasionally, if I hadn't paid attention at all, she would send me down the hall on an errand or, if the class got stuck, she would ask me for the right answer and then continue and let me lapse into my natural state of bovine curiosity. I moved at an incredibly rapid rate, internally, while the rest of me was lazy and content to sit in one spot for hours without moving.

We were opposites. I tore creation to bits with my questions, and isn't it, or is it, and then wondered why the world was made of so many parts. I continually asked, "Why? What's the reason for that? Why doesn't the earth fall into the sea, or is there a crutch under the moon that holds it up?" Whereas she . . . it wasn't that she mothered creation but she had accepted, quietly, in her womanly way, the continuity of existence and so life mothered her. There was a plenitude of milk. I also decided that she must love her husband very much, since she was so nice to me. And whenever I got the answer right she said nothing, but looked as if this was what she always expected. When I left the third grade, I never saw her again except once, accidentally, in the street when I imagined that she was disappointed by the nervousness she saw developing in me . . . but from her a chthonic, deep "yes" appeared in creation.

4

Within a few years, instead of idiot or dummkopf I heard, "Here comes the ugly Einstein." Then a pause. Then repeated in a childish chorus, "Here comes the ugly Einstein with her undershirt and glasses." In fact, I was neither ugly nor an Einstein but my mother dressed me in lumpy, shapeless clothes and my eyes were crossed under thick, pink glasses of the old-fashioned type which have just become popular again. In addition, I had two bristly, sausage-like braids so I thought I was doomed, whether I was an idiot or a genius, to be an outcast, and I decided that people would have to love me for my character. So deeply did the "ugly Einstein" myth take hold that many years later, when people told my mother what a beautiful daughter she had, she was never sure if they meant me or else decided that they hadn't looked at me closely. Her opinion of me always had a "but." I was intelligent "but" uncreative; I was not ugly "but" if you looked closely and so on . . . in short, she followed a law of rivals I have often observed. When two women are competitors, they often smell one another out without really knowing what the other looks like. They simply collect the other's traits into a hostile "her." And so my mother recognized me and fed me but never really knew what I looked like.

As I read, my other world developed limits and allies. For example, when I read about strange, philosophical systems—Plato's, for example—I thought that these men were just like me, always batting the air with their nonexistent concoctions. The only difference was that they were big and believed their twaddle whereas I was little, and kept mine to myself. But as soon as I read "the good of good," or whether red was red or some other thing that only gave birth to red, I knew I was in good company. However, when I heard that poor Socrates was hanging emaciated in a basket while his disciples moved around underneath uselessly, I thought that was overdoing things and perhaps he didn't love his wife and was just unhappy. No one told me what to read; but by the tone in which they mentioned an author, I instinctively knew if he was for me or a waste of time. There was only one thing wrong with the philosophers, I felt: they didn't have their sympathies in the right place. They wrote as if, in order to succeed, all you had to do was follow this or that rule, like climbing this or that ladder of right and wrong, whereas it seemed to me that life consisted of the possibility of defeat and my sympathies were with the poor and outcast. I understood, in my own way, Plato and Marx and the others very well. They were my brothers because they were all climbing ladders they had invented themselves, but they were arrogant.

So my friends became the artists, the novelists, and I read copiously as my eyes gulped a page at a time. I thought everyone did this until a neighborhood librarian asked me if I really finished the heap of books I took home each week and I said "yes," and showed her how I did it by going diagonally down the page twice and forming an "x" with my eyes. Together with Shakespeare and Tolstoy, I read dog stories or "The Adventures of Mottele," and I cried and laughed for hours about his exploits and how he got caught stealing apples in a Jewish ghetto somewhere in Eastern Europe.

I could always recognize Jewish writers by the way their characters went flying off into another world. I understood too well the impetus for that dream world, and when someone showed me a painting with characters and cows and moons all detached from the earth and headed for some imaginary point, I knew the painter was a Jew. So I cried for hours happily with Mottele, the little boy whose dreams were apples and hot rolls and starched, white blouses.

5

In our new house, our television room was oblong with a couch facing the screen. Opposite was a desk and lamp where my sister studied. Like my bedroom, the walls had been hand-plastered into clumps of green paint in the Spanish style. Frequently, while my mother was downstairs making apple pie or some other dessert you oughtn't to eat and it was very peaceful, my father rubbed my back or massaged my head for hours and only stopped to ask why I was too lazy to scratch his in return.

I can still feel the absolute warmth and luxury associated with all that rubbing . . . from which I got the tenacious idea that existence had the promise of pleasure. One writer says that beauty is, "La promesse du bonheur; the promise of happiness." For me it is the return to childhood, which is why it is so dangerous.

These massages, which frequently lasted three or four hours, were interrupted if a love scene appeared. At the slightest threat of physical touch, my father would get up, hitch his pants around his thickening waist, and leave the room. Sometimes he would say, "Well, Cookie, I have to pay someone a visit" or "I have to go see a little man," and then disappear into the bathroom or else simply vanish. He only returned when he had waited long enough to be sure the scene was over. His expression was a mixture of guilt, as if he personally had done something wrong, and embarrassment, like a little boy who looks and discovers that his pants have fallen down and wants to run away and hide. I explained this by the fact that he grew up in an orphanage, where people were rarely touched except to be hit.

In this way existence acquired, like a bed, the soft, pulling promise of pleasure.

6

I had my first actual conversation with the other world in the following way.

My father's face began to lose the flux that had made it so handsome and instead a mean look, and sluggish manner developed which greeted everything with, "No, and don't you smell too, if you catch yourself while you aren't looking," as his teeth and nostrils spread and there was an unhealthy, white mucous in the corners of his eyes. The handsome glow of youth and self-assurance, which had lighted up his simple, intelligent face, dimmed permanently.

One day my father was sitting on our Knabe piano stool in a foul humour of the sort that always ended in my being hit. "Here," he said, "if you want your allowance, beg." My allowance was a matter of a quarter a week which I spent on macaroni salad and bubble gum which I bought from an enormously fat woman at a neighborhood store. I thought of our dog who begged for his food and said, "No." "I'll teach you," my father replied, and hit me in the face. "Have you changed your mind?" he asked. "No," I said, "you can do what you want with my body—but you'll never touch my mind." Then he hit me again, until he finally got tired, and muttering something like, "You'll never be happy with any man," abandoned trying to educate me. I believe my mother gave me the money later.

A few weeks after that we were all sitting at the dinner table where these scenes frequently began, with an aunt and uncle from another town. I must have refused to say, "Yes, father," or something of the sort. In any case he hit me again, in the face, and then my uncle carried me upstairs.

As we went around the alcove with all the books which formed our library I, in his arms, had a little talk with Tolstoy. I was sure he would have understood that I was a good girl and

29

hadn't done anything wrong. I was deeply convinced of my integrity and felt I had finally found an ally.

Then I wrote a letter, which I sent downstairs via my uncle, telling my father that he ought not to treat a young lady that way; that he was lowering his dignity. My uncle read the letter and said in his passive, sedentary way, "The pen is mightier than the sword," took it downstairs. There was a moment of silence as my father read it aloud, and then said, "That's how she is. You can't do anything with her." The others were all quiet. By then the beatings were a well-established fact, like so-and-so's tick.

Meanwhile, upstairs, I had a private, wordless discussion with my friend. He was as real to me as anyone I knew and could see. As I cried, I thought of his invariable death scenes which always followed the same, satisfying pattern: "Prince So-and-So looked up at the sky, which a moment ago had been so clear, so blue, so full of expectation, and which was now filled with the remnant of gunpowder and the cries of the wounded. Then he looked down, and perceiving the hole in his belly, from which the blood flowed copiously, as if from someone else, who was, and was not, himself, Prince So-and-So mused, 'Is this death? Is this the great event? And what was I thinking of before when the important thing was to be a brave officer and lead my company into battle? How is it that I was unaware of this? Why did I not realize that what mattered was elsewhere, involved somehow in this event?' Prince So-and-So felt that only now, when it was too late, a veil was being lifted from his eyes."

I pictured Tolstoy as very tall and energetic, like Levin. Many years later I saw a picture of a shrivelled old man dressed like a Russian peasant with wild, cunning eyes, standing like a mushroom next to Gorky and I realized it was "he."

After my first conversation, it was only a small step to decide that these great writers never entirely died but handed down something of their spirits from generation to generation so that it never went entirely out of existence. Here is what I mean. I vaguely imagined Sophocles opening his palm and handing something material, but invisible, to Sappho, who gave it to Shakespeare, who gave it to Tolstoy, and so on.

Perhaps I had "The Creation of Adam" in mind, and the idea that these writers, like the Lord, also held out their palms in calm sorrow at the parting and creation of life. In any case, I thought of my concoction, even then, as a continuity of consciousness: that there was something precious that never left the human race. I believed in this, in the same way that you sense the presence of people who are gone around you; but I never spoke about it.

Instead, I decided that since Tolstoy was my ally, the kernel of integrity I had promised to defend was safe . . . but the distinction between my spirit and what they did to my body developed; a distinction, ironically, that must have sustained the Jews, or anyone else for that matter, in the concentration camps. I cried for hours with my friend, the fatherly great writer.

5

With her Renoir-like face, and thick, dark hair piled on top of her head like two pears in the style that was then fashionable, my mother prepared health-giving portions of meat and vegetables nightly in our kitchen, and then brought them into the green stucco alcove where we had dinner. She fed us as if we were going to be deprived momentarily so we had better store up. She ate by surrounding her plate with both her arms, to keep off the invader, and then gobbled whatever was there quickly. She looked up suspiciously from time-to-time, with an unpleasant clacking of her teeth which were still chewing, to make sure the terrain was clear. Then she attacked again and finished off all the morsels before anything could happen to them.

From this I realized that Jews have a deep fear of starving to death, which is why they eat all the time, with little pleasure but much satisfaction. Once the meal was over, she had again outwitted the enemy, who was only parescent in those days.

My father ate in a businesslike, matter-of-fact way in order to get done with a necessary function. When the meal was over, he forgot about it. My sister hardly ate: she was like a little bird that had fallen out of its nest onto the street and somehow managed to grow up. Her little wings seemed about to fold or give way altogether from an insufficient life force. She often complained to my mother about me, saying, "She hit me again, the bully." Then she cried. My sister did herself great damage by running to my mother instead of trying to defend herself by her own means. I was much taller and stronger than she, although I was only a year older.

I used my ten fingers, full force. If my mother slapped me for hitting my sister, I cried and then began again, until I felt the familiar, pleasant sensation which came from having had too much. Then I waited a while and began again, or snatched something from my sister's plate. From this healthy, bloated feeling I developed a habitual, cow-like sense of comfort which I associated with my braids and glasses.

After dinner my father went downstairs into a labyrinth of tools and mechanisms, many of which he had invented himself, and which were incomprehensible to me. The cellar had become his refuge, from which he only emerged to complain about the noise or something else that interfered with his work. Although I respected his intelligence and ability to work for hours without relief, I never understood the appeal of all these screwdrivers, and pliers, and plugs. It seemed to me that he was picking at time, trying to obfuscate it with all those clever gadgets, just as my mother did when she nibbled.

The first phase of the evening began when my mother sat down at our old Knabe piano, which only once in its long life ever got a tuning, and kept a constant, sweet tone in spite of all its abuse. The Knabe was immediately next to the kitchen so that we punctuated our songs with large plate fulls of this and that. My sister sat on one side and I on the other; my mother was in the middle on our wooden piano stool, so that there was frequent pushing and shoving for room.

Then my mother took out a disorderly bundle of those sensitive spirits who understood her, mainly Chopin and Beethoven, and began an étude with a look of deep spirituality which I have only seen when she watches ballet or plays the piano. Then out came the lonely, delicate Chopin, missing many of his teeth, it's true, as the expression of all her life wasn't and might have been. From time-to-time she got stuck in one of those toothless trills with their long, agonized tension, and nervous, lyrical release. Then she stopped, lifted a finger to relocate the guilty note and with a "Sheis, I go on," she found the note on the music sheet and drummed ahead to finish with the

33

same intense, spiritual look. Our metronome ticked away irrelevantly, since no one paid attention to it, and eventually we shut it off.

My mother was never daunted by the missing notes, or general cacophony; everything was patched together by the same spirituality, which was as sacred to her as good food, or money. Then finishing with, "Ach, how sensitive. Ja, Ja, if only I hadn't . . ." She would close Chopin, and take out the "Appasionata."

Here was a real field for action. She went ahead like a firetruck over its heights and despondency and charged over her own mistakes with, "Sheis," or, "Ach, mensch meier," and whirled and exhausted herself in these seductive, intensely lonely feelings which should have existed. The "Appasionata," too, came out like lightning, missing many of its teeth . . . but I tried not to listen. Chopin, I thought, was lonely and romantic but capable of satisfaction, whereas whoever wrote the "Appasionata" was desperate. I knew nothing about Beethoven's life, or that it was he who wrote the piece, but I sensed that it was unbearable. In fact, I frequently left the room when anyone played Beethoven's music, thinking to myself that no art was worth it.

It was always the mind, the creator behind the music, who appealed to me, like Tolstoy and his books. So I told my mother that I thought it was sad to be a performer and have your art die at the end of each piece when the audience left, and that the composer or writer moved me more because they were more permanent; I felt they served a different, more powerful instinct. In fact, I thought it would be a joy, a constant escape from pain to be a violinist and fiddle your way through life. For this reason, I sometimes told people that my father played the violin and we floated up and down the Danube in a boat, while he fiddled for our living.

My mother, however, looked at me as if I had somehow appeared from the garbage can and just happened to be her daughter and said, "Ach, such a cold child. With no feeling for humanity. It is the most beautiful thing—to play, to dance, to express yourself."

Then with her bony, arthritic fingers still on the piano, she usually began to cry. "If I didn't have children I might have . . . but now I am trapped in this house. Be sure girls that you never do the same thing. Make your own lives first so no one can tell you what to do."

Then she pointed her little nose up into the air and hopeless, ineffective tears kept coming. The world was like a cup filled with tears, which was being tipped over so that they spilled out and the earth was depleted. I wished I was a man who could do something. I hated my mother for making me feel guilty that I had been born. And, as always, I had a horrible feeling of physical repulsion for her weakness and for her flesh itself. Then I listened for the sequel. "Girls, you are the best thing in my life, the best thing I have done. I love you more than anything else on earth. I'm very proud of you. Never forget that." Then I stopped listening; the cup was empty.

"If only I hadn't married that monster," she went on, "that insensitive beast, but I want . . . for my children . . . Once in Germany, before the war, I met a young doctor and we went bicycling in shorts and sneakers. It was beautiful, summer, and he was so nice, gentle. He brought me presents and I think he wanted to marry me. He was a doctor so he had a good income, but then the war came and he disappeared. I think sometimes, I don't know, that I would have been . . ." The cup broke and I decided that I would tell her nothing.

Then she got up with her rear going, as usual, in the wrong direction and returned from the kitchen with a plate of carrots and celery and chocolate. "Eat this," she said, "it's good for the eyes." Or, "You need some calories after all, it ties the system together." In this way, art and screaming and eating were all in a heap in my mind so that I could do all three, or any two, all at once with no sense of collision.

Then the second phase of the evening began.

In spite of the fact that one part of her went circuitously around the other with no respect for the laws of kinesthetics or grace, my mother felt that she could have been a great dancer. "If only they hadn't put me on toe shoes, the idiots, when my bones were still soft and now I have flat feet. They ruined me." Reality, however, and the fact that she looked like a dancing gorilla made no inroad on her dream, and my sister was to become the great dancer in her place. (A dancer recreated the seductive, unobtainable feelings that my mother had never expressed in her own life. She was infinitely remote, and infinitely desirable to an audience that was always distant. In this way, her nature found its exact niche in a performing art.)

So almost every evening we played Bach, or the most serious classical music we had, and my sister put on a black leotard from which her skinny little limbs stuck out awkwardly, each going its own way like a duck, as is often true of young children. Then my mother's eyes gleamed with a demonic, frantic look which was at the same time intensely spiritual, and the music climbed and climbed until it seemed to cry out, "Holy, holy, holy," as the great genius confronted death, or the terminus of his own passion. At these moments, as her arms and legs tried to follow the overflowing motion of the fugues, the same look of spirituality and concentration appeared on my sister's apprehensive, frightened face. But just when the idealism—which is, after all, the expectation of sympathy and likeness in others—should have carried her along and connected all the parts of her underdeveloped body, at that very moment, as the tension and light in the music climbed toward its height and then rang out consistently with a sustained peal, "Holy, holy, holy," her little wings drooped, and folded, and flapped around as if searching for a center and her expression seemed to say, "I'm afraid to go on. What if no one's looking."

When the music was over my mother hugged my sister tightly and said, "What a queen. You are wonderful. So creative. You must be a great dancer and to hell with them. Ach! So wonderful." A tiny bit of saliva rolled from the crowns in my mother's mouth onto my sister's pale, uncertain cheek.

Toward midnight I was reading with my nose and glasses directly under the lamp so that the light would not spread—my father had forbidden me to read after ten o'clock—when my sister turned around in bed and said, opening her large eyes with their enormous silver-grey shadows which were unusual for such a young girl, and in contrast to her cheerful freckles, "Moo told me she tried to have an abortion of me today. But it didn't work." She stared at me and then at the wall with her

36

habitual, lost, ragamuffin expression. "Don't believe her," I answered, for once forgetting about myself, "She's just trying to be mean."

Then she said, flapping her arms over the blanket in the detached, plastic way young children have of moving their limbs, "She said she didn't want me." My sister didn't cry; if she had been able to cry, she would have been saved. Instead she just continued to stare in the vague bedroom light that reached her, as if she just happened to be there and might just as well be somewhere else, or nowhere at all. I thought to myself that my mother was a thorough technician. But I wondered, looking at the grey-green shadows which were even deeper in the dim lamplight, where the motive for all this destruction came from.

Then wearing my white-flannel nightgown with blue and green flowers, I put on long, red-knitted slippers with leather soles and went downstairs to get something to eat. I called this nocturnal munching, during which I frequently met my mother, the "refrigerator patrol." My mother always had a bizarre expression on her face when I found her nibbling a little non-fattening this-or-that, like a squirrel snatching an acorn, nervously, from a tree before anyone can frighten it from its perch. However, I was used to a great deal of quackerie in my house.

On that particular evening, still in his red-flannel blouse and grey worker's pants, my father stood in the alcove where we ate and raised his thick, powerful arm over my mother as if he were about to hit her with all the force of his broad, muscular body. In spite of the fact that his nostrils flared and his eyes glowed like two small, malevolent points, and the veins stood out on his neck as he held his arm threateningly over her, I still felt an edge of intelligent self-control in him. His expression said, "Better be careful, or you might injure yourself or the furniture. Or, with all her ideas of women's rights, she might call the police." So his arm shook the air and he said, "I'll teach you." His most destructive actions were always accompanied by a mysterious, educational purpose which took the form of, "This is for your good," or, "You have to learn," or, "This too will pass." I thought that the murderer needed to justify himself.

My mother, however, recoiled as if she had been hit, with a hysterical, cold look in her face like a trapped animal that knows it is weaker and has to defend itself through cunning. She took a can of partly melted orange juice and hurled the liquid at him, saying, "Damn you, you beast." The liquid splattered his shirt, his pants, and splashed onto the green-stucco wall.

Although his arm was still raised and trembled with its own force, the edge of awareness dominated, or else the inability to hit an equal. In any case, my father lowered his arm and wiped away the juice. More and more, I thought that what drove him was the need to assert his absolute authority; once that was done and the victim was terrified, the actual beating was secondary.

As I turned around and went up the bannister, I heard:

"You're poisoning the children's minds against me."

"Well, they're my children, you beast."

"I'll show you, with all your crack-pot ideas of women's rights which are just an excuse for . . ."

"You have ruined my life, you brute."

"And you are headed for the nut-house. By the way, I hear they have other lunatics there so you won't be alone."

I passed by the alcove filled with Shakespeare, and Marx, and the Rights of Everybody and got into bed. I promised to love my husband very much . . . but reality seemed remote, far away from my house, on the other side of this knife-blade of trouble.

6

"The Rosenbergs," I heard my mother say, late one evening in
autumn, with the frantic, determined gleam in her eye which
she reserved for music and martyrs as she put on a wool coat
and grey, knitted wool gloves. "Hurry up . . . they are going to
kill them tonight and I want my daughters to see . . . the injus-
tice. We have to get to Union Square or we will miss it. There's
a big electric clock and X, the leader, a terrific man, will give a
speech, also the wife of the other one they locked up. The
tyrants. I want you to see what life is. Here. Take a token each
and hold my hand so we don't get lost. Anne. What's the matter
with you? Why are you poking when it's a terrible event. Susan.
Put a sweater on underneath your coat or you'll catch cold and
watch out for the police. There are spies everywhere, even if
they look normal, but we have to go. They are killing them for
nothing. Two such innocent . . . angels . . . I will show you the
letters they wrote to each other in prison. There's a song, too.
Ach. Mench meier. Stop eating or we will miss it. At midnight
they are going to kill them in the electric chair." In this way, my
mother rushed us both out of the house and we hurried in the
subway to Union Square in downtown Manhattan.

When we arrived, a black mass, like smelted metal, moved
with latent turbulence and hysteria over a large area that was
surrounded by enormous clothing stores and powerful electric
lights. The mass moved indefinitely, but constantly, under a
huge electric clock that showed "11:35" in clear numbers

39

formed by bright bulbs and then, alternately, the temperature. Twenty-five minutes remained. To the right of the clock, on a high wood platform which was raised so that they would be visible to the entire crowd, were two small boys, my own age, who, as they stood with uncomprehending, passive expressions and the glazed eyes of children who sense, but do not understand, what is happening to them, reminded me of Mottele and his stolen apples and dreams. They were small, skinny boys with dark hair and clean, intelligent faces. "Orphans," I thought to myself, "in twenty-five minutes they will be orphans . . . and who put them up there like that?" It wasn't right that they should be exposed, but there was something wrong with the whole crowd. I felt it the moment I arrived, as I saw thousands of people pushing against the barricades set around the square by the police, who also moved with slow, threatening gestures.

As the clock showed the advance of each minute, a slender woman, the wife, apparently, of the third man who had been given a life sentence and then put in jail with the criminal, not political prisoners, stood up beside the boys on the platform and spoke in a steady, high, feminine voice as she made a plea for amnesty for her husband. Soon she was followed by another, deeper Negro voice. I can't remember whether it was a man or woman singing. The crowd began to pulse as if the molten metal was about to pour out and burn its container, as the deep black voice started, without an introduction and my mother said, "Listen. They wrote this for them in prison."

"Oh, if I could sing, oh, what would I sing,
   my loved one?
Oh, if I could sing, oh, what would I sing,
   my loved one,
The earth and sky, they rumble by,
Oh, what would I sing, my loved one?"

The clock read 11:49 as the voice continued; it continued to sing out, clear and defiant, as the crowd pushed and the metal grew hotter. When the clock read midnight, in blazing white bulbs, I had the feeling that my own flesh was melting and I

40

began to cry convulsively, uncontrollably, as I looked up at the two orphans who stood there, silent, motionless like two little tooth-picks. "Why did they bring them here?" I thought to myself. "It's not right." The singing had stopped and a dreadful wail, like a woman who has just lost her lover and holds out useless, barren arms in the darkness, broke out. On the other side of the barriers, the police moved incessantly, with a clear threat in the wood clubs and guns they carried on their hips. At the same time, another voice from the platform, apparently it was X, the leader of the entire left, urged the crowd to act with restraint and dignity, in a manner worthy of the Rosenbergs who were no longer alive.

The molten metal, however, irrespective of the rational, intelligent voice on the platform, moved and pulsed with increasing violence as I stood there, crying. I don't know where so many tears came from. "It isn't right," I thought, "they are innocent . . . but the crowd is exactly the same, only in reverse." I couldn't explain what I meant, but the huge sobbing mass around me was doing precisely the same thing as those who killed the Rosenbergs, but against itself. And I hated my mother passionately, consistently, for bringing me there.

As I stood in the vast, amorphous darkness, which was filled by a mob that held still another black threat and purpose, I felt that some essential innocence was being violated, that the world could never compensate for what had just been done. I wondered if they blindfolded them when they tied their hands to the electric chair. "Were the straps made of leather or metal?" I asked myself. "What if the current missed and there was an empty click?" Then I heard my mother's voice, "Sheis. The bastards. She asked to be killed first, and they couldn't do it. There wasn't enough electricity." A fat woman in a dirty kerchief came over to my mother, crying. "They had to kill her twice," she said, whispering into my mother's ear, as if she was afraid the police would hear. "Ach, the tyrants," my mother said. "Girls, never forget this. They killed them. Innocent. Martyrs."

I had the recurrent feeling that my own flesh, open and defenseless, had just been violated.

41

7

In a rare moment of simultaneous accord, in which politics and peace were pushed, like winter, to a remote part of things, my mother picked up a pair of pruning shears and rubber gloves and my father tightened his belt and the entire family migrated to our yard. There everything was abundance as the lilacs and roses of all colors grew beside the metal fence that separated our garden from our neighbors and covered the little triangle it formed with hot, opening plenitude. Lavender and red and yellow and orange all lined the geometric fence as, feeling the happy weight of my protuberant stomach, I said, "Flowers are the most beautiful thing there is." My father looked at me with his mixture of pride and distrust, as he usually did when I proclaimed about something abstract or unseen, and then remarked to the inobservant air, "There she goes."

With her hair piled on top of her bobbing head, my mother hitched up her halter and adjusted her shorts which, like the rest of her vestitory combination, predated the last World War together with the heroic efforts of the women who survived it. Then carefully putting on her rubber gloves to make sure the second stage of the dire dialectic, in the form of arthritis and the coal stoves which Hitler had prevented her parents from heating, would not strike and upset the delicate equilibrium of her inner parts, she bent down and quietly cut and weeded our healthy lawn. Happily she clacked her teeth and cut the grass that grew at the base of the opulent rose bushes and worked silently at her task for hours. The daily, dual stage of the ominous theory receded to a winter background, together with rheumatism and the omnipresent threat of insufficiency. As she clipped and cut, there was a contrapuntal knocking to balance the children who were in the front part of the garden. Then there was unabstract peace as, melodically, mellifluously, the entire mechanism of the fateful dialectic slipped a notch and slid deceptively, into its early stage of stasis and silent work.

"Ach, mench meier," yelled my mother in vibrant Teutonic tones such as the Vikings, or Goths, or Visigoths might have produced when setting forth on a voyage of subjugation. "Dat is der Plumshon." This meant "little plum" in my mother's private compound of English and German, and referred to our dog, whose hind quarters sank in canine martyrdom from my weight onto the thick rug of green grass below. "What a mench," yelled my father happily from the front yard as I continued to dig my belly into the poor dog's ribs. Pug, meanwhile, looked at me with his beautiful, chestnut eyes as he sank deeper and deeper into the grass in his red and white tuxedo as if imploring me, with dog-like understanding and mercy, not to treat him like a horse. Suddenly, however, as I heard, "cold, unfeeling child," muttered into the benign rose bushes together with a subsequent lowering of the nose and other disapprobatory indications, Der Plumshon forgot his human tendencies and deposited me in a heap as a black ball sped across the grass to the back alley. Gone was charity and anthropoid indulgence; he was all Pug. "Oh, ho," laughed my father, hitching up his belt around his red-check lumberjack shirt as I got up from the grass and Muffet, our cat, out did Pug. "A real mench," he repeated. This was his highest form of approbation and one I only heard applied to our dog. No one else ever fully qualified. Shakespeare and Marx occasionally got close, but only Pug entered into the canon of truly heroic endurance and stamina.

"Let's go," he said a few minutes later, as he took the car keys out of his pocket. My mother, meanwhile, munching her teeth and calculating to herself the result of her dialectic-defeating portions of yesterday's supper, finished pruning a small patch of weeds, which grew under a wonderfully thick, red cluster of rose bushes along the grey, wire fence. "Giddy-up," said my sister, turning her little sunflower face up toward the light as she rode on top of Pug without actually sitting on him. She was much lighter than I, and she succeeded in making him go around the garden and under the lilacs as she held his collar like reins.

"Giddy-up, giddy-up," she repeated as the unsteady elements in her tottering nature were held in balance by the sun, the lilacs, and the momentary absence of disequilibrium.

Then we all got into the green Plymouth whose grill looked like my father's face and had a thick layer of mechanical life, and I climbed in the front seat. "I have to be careful of Sunday drivers," my father said. This referred to women, alcoholics, and artists, all of which he placed in the same, useless category. And then we were off: to adventure, and food, and the hidden, Sunday innuendo of a vast, cement metropolis.

8

"Come on Cookie," my father said one afternoon in a voice swelling with inner approbation and dogs, "I just did it." This meant that I would have to stand in a specific, mysterious position. These were the early days of high-fidelity when you had to approximate yourself to the music, and listen to something I liked even less. "I can't," I replied from my little nest under the green, stucco alcove.

"I want you to hear it," he repeated, with a squaring edge of pride. So realizing that I would give in, I went down the spiral bannister and into the living room where my father was bent down on his knees, in front of a veritable orchestra of speakers, and asked where I should stand. "Not there," he said, indicating with reaches of canine puff, that I was not square in the center, "to the left, there, that's it."

"But I don't like it," I said, feeling the comforting weight of my stomach and remarking to myself, forever, that people would have to love me for my character. "Okay, stay there," he repeated, in a tone that bagged forth on tune and landed happily at the end of the bars. "I have just finished perforating all the speakers—there are three systems altogether—and I want to test the reproduction." The living room rug was covered by these systems, which represented the latest discoveries in musical sound and contained nine speakers each; even the walls vibrated, not to speak of our neighbors. My father had just finished making individual holes in the black felt material of which the speakers were made and had consequently placed a megacycle tester, a machine similar in efficacy to our metronome, in front of one of the systems so that he could measure the distortion or accuracy of his equipment. This testing process and the subsequent swirling crescendoes would continue for at least three hours. He no longer listened to the music; it was the mechanical reproduction that interested him.

"I'm there," I said, unhappily depositing my stomach like a snail, in a new spot.

"No, move to the right."

"Where?"

"To the right, in the center. Okay. Now listen." At this point, music appropriate to ghosts and goblins came on, even though it was only the afternoon. At the same time, my father bent down over the megacycle tester so that there was a collateral banging between the two, and I wanted to escape.

"It's too loud," I said.

"Sheis," came from the kitchen, in a tone of injured sensitivity and apple pies, "Ich cannish." The end of the flour-filled epithet was lost in the oven as "A Night on Bald Mountain" whirled to a finale, dragging its megacycle-defying depths with it, and then there was a deceptive pause in our living room.

"Wait, Cookie," he said without looking up. After the noise, something sad would appear. "I want to make sure the deep notes are properly registered." My father's intelligence and ability to scrutinize his own efforts, however, were lost because he had no idea how to market his own production. Then he turned on the testing machine which sent its sonorous din out through our green-stucco walls and over the rose bushes until it was lost in the vast, encyclopedic ignorance of our neighbors.

"Oh, no," I thought, as the machine boomed and the most unhappy music I had ever heard came on loud, blasting away as if it were returning from a Napoleonic war at the head of a band of cripples and hopeless wounded.

"I don't want to listen," I said, hearing the soul-cracking solitude of the composer.

"There she is again," my father remarked, sincerely disappointed that I was going up the stairs.

"No art is worth it," I replied, and hurried back under my

46

alcove where I took out my incipient other world. I knew the sequel. My father transferred himself to the theoretical center of the room together with all his equipment, and for the next few hours until dinner time, the megacycles boomed together with Beethoven, until there was a fugue-like agony in our house which lasted and soared, full of high-fidelity reproduction, out into the deaf neighborhood around us.

9

When summer had really come, we parked our car, which was filled with what we would need for the next three months, at the bottom of a long path lined with moss and stones and salamanders which came out in the rain. This was in a pine forest with a clear, fresh-water lake. My father loaded the tent, which was too heavy for one man, onto his back and went up the hill. I went up after him when my mother had loaded pots and pans, and lanterns and silverware, and whatever else she could find room for, on my plump, sturdy back and shoulders. Each year we followed the same path, which had been worn into black, rich soil by myriad families, until we passed a communal, metal water pump which, together with the latrine, was our only help from civilization. Higher and higher we went, until finally we found a campsite that seemed insulated from the wind and thunder. It was very important to choose the proper point at which to fasten the large tarpaulin to the ground, otherwise the hurricanes would wash away everything and leave us without a roof. Then my father dropped the canvas to the ground sluggishly, and stretched and complained about an ache in the small of his back. A dislocation that eventually made him unable to work began on these trips when he carried the tent himself.

However, the air, the virgin pine trees, the moist fertile earth, everything was crawling with its own life and growth. So we dug a steep ditch around the area where we would put the tent, in order for the rain to run off down the hill. Next, it was time to hoist the tent itself. Still sweating and complaining about his back, my father went to get our neighbors. It was impossible for one man to raise the tent by himself, so there was an unwritten rule, which everyone obeyed, that the men help one another. Within a few minutes our neighbors, whom we hadn't seen since the summer before, came laughing and swearing. They wiped their moustaches to remove a real or imaginary trace of beer and tucking their shirts over their round, protuberant bellies and placing several cans of beer on stones near-by, they grabbed the stakes and lifted the large tarpaulin onto the main pole which my father held as we three watched. The tent had to be properly balanced in the center, sunk securely into the earth, and then properly attached by wooden pegs at the side, otherwise it might fall over while the men were away working in the city.

"One, two, three, hup," they said, and then, "We did it," and, "Let's have some beer," as the tent stood nicely balanced on the main pole, its graceful walls curving onto the little stakes at each lower seam.

Then these heavy, Italian men placed their bellies carefully over a stone, as if they were proud of all creation and particularly of their stomachs, and lighting cigars or cigarettes, wiped the sweat off their faces and underarms and rubbed their dirty pants. Then they opened several cans of beer with a loud snap, letting the foam run on the earth. My father would not touch the beer, which was in the domain of embarrassing television scenes and other unmentionable activities, but I decided that when I grew up I would drink beer and ruminate like a man. I imagined myself with a big belly and a moustache, and more important, with their assurance of sweaty, masculine dominion.

Soon my father, laughing and content because of his own strength, and because his old friends were sitting around him and had not forgotten him, said that if he wanted to get the "fly" up before dark, he had to go back to work. The "fly" was a long, sturdy strip of canvas which ran the length of the front of the tent and was attached to the trees with ropes to form a protective shell which became our kitchen. Later we added mosquito nets and canvas flaps, so that the entire area in front of the tent was sheltered. Once the tent and the "fly" were up, the most difficult work was over. We all agreed to meet later that evening at a campfire, in a clearing beside the lake.

So all afternoon we tied the fly to the sturdy pine and birch trees on which it hung, and unpacked the kerosene stoves, and filled the kerosene lanterns, and put in new wicks. Then we unpacked our clothes, and stored them in wood crates under white canvas cots inside the tent. Finally when it was dark, my father said we were finished and the rest would have to wait for the following day.

Then he took out our green lantern which he had previously filled, and pumped it until it could hold no more pressure. He lifted the glass and lit the wick, whose white mesh immediately caught and flared very brightly with an intense blue-white light which turned yellow as he reduced the flow of kerosene. How beautiful the lantern was, as the mosquitoes and butterflies came in small finger-fulls, and then crashed against its metal top and fell to the earth. The small, powerful light had a peculiar glow and warmth which spread over our kitchen, where my mother was preparing dinner, and vanished in the audible, sweet blackness that surrounded our tent.

When we had carried pails of water up from the pump along the path, we did the dishes and then combed our hair in front of mirrors hanging from the pine and birch trees that supported the fly. Then we walked to a clearing next to the lake, which gleamed like liquid metal in the beautiful, summer night. Overhead there were myriad constellations, like fireflies, as the men built a bonfire of bricks they had piled together; then we roasted marshmallows and frankfurters on green strips of birch.

One of our friends had grown five inches and developed pimples, another was a busy medical student, and still another was married and sitting next to his plump wife. Only the adults were the same.

The master of ceremonies, his stout, hairy legs sticking out from shorts as if he had something to hide, laughed loudly at his own jokes, as if to prove in that way that they were funny, and lit a pipe. Then he called, in turn, on all those who were known to have good voices, or a noisy trick.

Finally it was my turn. I got up slowly, feeling a distinct, placid satisfaction from my stomach which was filled with marshmallows. I chose a song my father had taught me in his nocturnal chanting before I went to sleep, although I knew it would bore the audience who would only tolerate a pretty, childish voice. I sang:

In the gloaming, oh my darling,
When the lights are dim and low,
And the quiet shadows falling,
Softly come and softly go . . .

My voice obeyed me, and rose and held the high notes when I needed them as if there was an involuntary accord between it and me.

It went still higher. I looked up and felt my spirit soar, rise, and reach for those vast, impartial constellations which were like lighted swarms of mosquitoes which would exist, apart from human need or desire, forever, long after I was dead.

10

Under an alcove which he had plastered by hand with green-paint on a sponge, producing a Spanish, stucco effect, my father constructed a large secretary in my bedroom, by placing an unvarnished plank of wood on top of two wooden drawers. In front of this oval, I looked each day to see if the two pimple-like things on my chest had progressed, and each day it was the same; there was no change. What wasn't there refused to move. When this probing inside my nasty undershirt and the subsequent disappointment had continued for about a year, I decided that I was a hopeless case and would never be a woman. In addition to my nothing, I had two apish braids which at the slightest provocation, stuck out to the four winds like a hellenic curse, and old-fashioned pink eyeglasses. In addition, my mother still dressed me like a German school maiden, all of which made me dread the moment when the boys at school would put their hands on my undershirt straps, which you could feel beneath my clothing, and shout out, for the whole class to hear, "The ugly Einstein. Here's the ugly Einstein in her under-shirt." Children have the knack of sniffing out your most secret fear and obsession, and then advertising it to the four corners.

One night, after the usual fear at school, I had the following dream.

I saw a molten, lava-like mass of incredibly bright, intense reds and blacks and yellows which all ran together to form a volcanic river which was flooded with its own pourings of hot, oilish matter, and which in turn gouged a deep path along a black, chthonic mountainside which was receptive and resistant at the same time. Then in an inhuman burst of energy, the colors fused and melted and shook apart in a burst of dazzling yellow and heat. Then instantly, just as when you are in a lighted room and suddenly someone turns out the light and for a moment you are not sure you still exist; in the same way, the explosion was followed by a pocket of blackness which was, and was not myself, and during which I somehow managed to exist in an insensate, exhausted state.

This emptiness seemed prophetic and I was frightened of the repetitive motif in all these dreams of remaining sensate, alive, although I was dead. I woke up for a moment, looked at the darkness, and then immediately went back to sleep. After this dream, I felt even more like a lonely nucleus in a shell that did not fit.

My feeling of isolation from myself made me fly to a land of endless tenderness. In that division, which can also produce murders and severe disturbance because of its internal separation, lyricism is born. So the space between my soaring imagination and inadequate body, combined with the more and more frequent beatings I received at home, destroyed my intelligence and I flew into rages, like a hurricane.

TIME

If time is the distance between events—a definition I invented in high-school—then formerly it was the slow, peaceful vacuum of the characters' lives as I spent entire afternoons and evenings lying on the sofa in our television-room, reading. Whether I read Shakespeare, or de Maupassant, or Winnie-the-Pooh, time was suspended, or rather, it was like the notes of a lute. Why a lute, exactly? Because it's old, too, like time.

For example, the same notes can be played quickly or slowly or in different moods, and still the unit, the song, is the same. With sufficient alteration, the song may not even be recognizable . . . but I am getting off the track again. The fact is that I lost the ability to live in the characters' lives, the notes became cacophonous, and at the same time my almost photographic memory disappeared. Formerly I had learned whole charts at a gulp, or read a whole page at a time going diagonally down, from left-to-right, with my eyes. That feeling of innocent lucidity, in short, the urge to know, vanished.

So what did time become, if "time" is a thing, but periods of nervousness, slashed by blind spots when I was beaten and lapses of dreamy equilibrium when I planned and plotted in the future. Yet all these changes, like the original distance between events, took place in me, just as the notes occur in a fixed area called "the song." But that was slippery too; the song altered, the lute disappeared, I altered . . . but I can see a puddle coming.

When I could no longer stand the fear of being touched on my shoulders—on that horribly sensitive spot where my undershirt strap was and the invariable, "Here's the ugly Einstein. Here's the ugly Einstein," in a weird, childish sing-song—I went to Woolworth's and from among a long row of white, feminine items, I looked for the smallest brassiere in existence. When I managed to find one that was sub-zero, and in fact the size of two thimbles, I still knew I was going to have trouble. Then I paid for it, put the stringy, white thing in my brown, leather briefcase and took it home to the green alcove in my bedroom to see in what condition I was. I discovered that what I did not have was nevertheless larger on the left than on the right side and so the air pockets in my new item were not going to match. There was a revealing concavity on the right, and to tell the truth, that side was entirely empty except for the natural curve of my chest and the puffiness in the cloth. I didn't know what to do because the crushed part would certainly show under my sweater and everyone would know the truth, that I was wearing an empty rag, since no one is formed like a sponge.

So I worried; but nothing does not come from nothing, as they say in Latin, so I went to the medicine cabinet and pulled off two chunks of antiseptic cotton which I then molded to fit between me and my new item. That, however, was only the beginning of my troubles.

Soon these two miserable lumps, as my father would have called them, degenerated to a yellow-grey, unhealthy looking color which had the promise of internal growth. In addition, I decided that they had a special adaptability to my shape and so I was terrified that they would fall out, or that in some other way I would lose them. So each day, instead of myself, I inspected them for flying tufts or smelled to see if there was anything strong developing. Then I put them carefully in a white envelope which I tied with a rubber band, and hid the whole package in the secretary drawer.

I was terrified that some revealing hollow would show so that it would be obvious that I had added to things, and the equally strong conviction that these two declining pads had a unique fit, so what would I do if they shredded to bits. Meanwhile, my chest retained its two pimples and the mealy, disintegrating fibers formed shreds which fell off. I was ashamed of what I was doing and terrified of being caught by my father, who became insane if he caught me with it on. In fact, he did what the boys at school did, he put his hands on my shoulders or on my back, which in the process became excruciatingly sensitive, like an open wound, and if the straps were there, he turned into a wild animal which has lost all reason and has a hungry, moon-like look.

One evening when my mother was away, my father announced that the three of us would go to a cafeteria of the type where the food is put in steaming metal containers for hours until it has lost all flavor, and is served to you, from behind, by a sweating, underpaid worker. It was a place where local beggars and veterans, in horrible states of decay, went to meet and commiserate. This was after the war, when you saw these legless and armless creatures and sometimes worse, who have now died off, begging in the streets and then meeting their companions at the local cafeteria. This type of restaurant originated in New York City, where it was especially suited to the poor and itinerant who wanted a warm place to eat in a hurry. It was part of the vocabulary of the poor, and as such I hated it, because I could never look at these wretches without at the same time being ashamed that I was alive; that I ate, slept, etcetera, while "they" existed, and that my family never did

55

anything of quality. I used to think, when I saw these creatures, "How can they and I exist on the same earth? How is it possible?" And I still think, if anyone asked me about God, I would point to those basket cases . . . but to get back to the point, I asked my father, please, to take us somewhere else, anywhere, but not with all those bums and beggars. He, who was always on the way to the nonexistent poorhouse himself, said, "Well, the rich don't stink no worse. We'll go to the Horn and Harduct. The food won't poison you, and besides, we're poor people."

My father needed to identify with the poor so he could hate everyone else, or perhaps it was some nagging bond with his mother, or the inability, in spite of his natural intelligence, to imagine living differently than he always had. (All change begins with an act of imagination; I am here, poking along in my usual way, but I could be there, where it's all quite different.)

During the days and at school, I still wore my undershirt, but in the evening I would have preferred anything, even staying at home in my room, to the unendurable humiliation of leaving the house without it. I felt naked and horribly exposed unless I had the two straps in front of me, which for their part, had so degenerated that I had to safety-pin them together. Even then, there was the risk that the shreds would detach themselves and the entire contraption fall to my waist. The only thing I can liken the sensation to is the feeling you have after your face has been slapped in front of company and is still stinging. I felt that the entire area of my breasts and back had been violated.

My father, on the other hand, acquired the expression of an animal about to pounce on its prey and devour it if he suspected that I was wearing my secret item. His nostrils flared, making his nose seem disproportionately large, in fact, it seemed to take over and dominate his entire face; his eyes glittered with snake-like malevolence and his features spread apart as, for once, he lost all awareness of the consequences of his actions. Like a mad animal that needs to glut its hunger, he was obsessed by touching me on that terribly sensitive spot on my back to feel if the straps were there, and then he prepared for attack. Losing sight of everything except the urge to devour his victim and watch it bleed, with the proviso, in my case, that I

56

remain alive so he could return and attack again, he told me to take the thing off and be quick about it, otherwise he "would give it to me." I, meanwhile, had decided to fight for my spirit, even if I could not defend my body and I said, "It's not your concern. You have no right to interfere. It's a woman's matter."

We were standing outside our iron gate while the winter sun was just setting, with disappearing streaks of a grey, charcoal pencil, as I watched his expression change from the wish to destroy to the equally frightening look of satisfied lust. I didn't know what was happening to my father, all I knew was that he needed me alive to return for more, and that I had to be prone, absolutely motionless during these attacks, or he might have lost all sense of reason.

When the attack passed, his features acquired a taciturn, withdrawn look as they fell back into their grey, fleshy niches, and I went upstairs to take off my brassiere. I noticed more and more that my father needed to exercise arbitrary, absolute power. The actual violence, or physical injury to his victim, was secondary.

During the evening as we ate with the beggars, I consoled myself with the thought that the others, those indefinite, "others," who were always afloat in my brooding consciousness, would understand and know I was a good girl.

11

One afternoon I stood in front of a grey, spinsterish building in mid-Manhattan which looked as if it had folded its stony, dungeon-like arms many centuries before, during the crusades or some other period of torture, and retreated permanently into itself. Although it was only a girl's high school, there were stern, repressive grills over the windows. The stairway landings were barred against potential misdemeanors by massive iron railings which extended from the ceiling to the floor, and you entered through vast iron doors that clanged shut behind you. This reminded me of what I had noticed before: schools are like prisons. Punishment and education lead to the same architecture.

The atmosphere was completed, in fact, given subtle definition, by the very French, very malicious Madame Jones who, as ill-luck would have it, administered the entrance examination. This was Hunter College High School. Once a year, any girl who lived in New York City and was recommended by her principal could take the test; that was in the days, which are now disappearing, when a poor girl, by her wits, could still be educated entirely free by the state.

Then Madame Jones, with whom I was to suffer through four years of useless French verb books, and vulgar, ill-smelling powder—or rather powder that hid something ill-smelling—patted her tidy, grey, lifeless chignon, as if to suggest that we were all idiots who couldn't possibly be as refined as she, or really get anything right. Then she explained, with

58

wildly rolling "r"s and false teeth, how to take the examination in such a way that you understood absolutely nothing and despised education in general. The assumption was that there was an undefinable "it"—"eet"—at a new level of subtlety, that was French, difficult, and forever unattainable by us. Underneath her incessant gesticulation, as she battered the air with imaginary forks and knives and dimwitted finesse, was a stupid, unhappy woman who was incapable of doing anything but repeating herself.

Earlier that morning, with his two incredibly yellow eyes glowing—I often wondered how anyone with such yellow eyes could continue to live—Mr. Rowen, our principal, had placed a piece of paper with the four subway changes and two tokens in my hand. "Good-luck," he said, with tired, red veins beneath all the yellow, "No one has ever been accepted and you're our best hope. Work quickly, don't pay attention to the others, and don't think too much." For four years, I was then in the final year of grammar school, his worm eyes had followed me with a resigned, paternal air, as if to say, "I know very well what nastiness is going on here, but there is nothing I can do. In fact, you would make less trouble for yourself if you would leave things as they are and not try to fight for nonexistent causes. And I know how lonely you are. Don't think that I don't. But there's nothing I can do." I imagined that he understood me, although he contented himself with patching whatever malice and cunning he could not avoid noticing with an air of tired idealism. I often hoped he had a nice wife because he seemed so quiet and defeated. His eyes, with their dark, ochre shadows, reminded me of a living room with a brown rug and a warm fire which emitted red and yellow sparks. I imagined he was telling me, wordlessly, persistently, as he cautioned me about losing my way between trains, "See. Here's your change. You might be able to get out of here. There, over there in that other world, you will find people like yourself, and hope, and I will be able to say that at least one student of mine . . ."

Then I heard the rolling "r"s, as Madame Jones waved back and forth a mechanical pencil designed specifically for these computerized tests, and explained to us how and where we were to make an "eex," with a horrible mispronunciation of the

"x," as if it were a candy, a marron glacé, or something like that, which she was chewing and would spew in our direction. The implication was that we were too stupid to get the "eex" in the right place, so she would strain herself uselessly and explain it ten times, in the hope that we would realize that the machine did not know our minds.

As I sent several private "to hells" in her direction, I prepared myself through an internal hunching of all my latent faculties for what I called "the bomb mentality." This consisted of forgetting everything else and going ahead like a jet until I got to the end. I had understood long ago that these tests had nothing to do with reality and that in order to succeed, I had to guess what answer those who made the test wanted and then give it to them without thinking.

When Madame Jones said, "Begin," I remembered another test we had to take a few months earlier at school.

I knew everything, but in order to make sure, I peeked under my wooden desk and cheated. I looked a few words up in a dictionary, but I had them right too. Later on, the others who had seen me made fun of me but I explained to them that I hadn't changed anything. I just happened to know all the words.

When I heard that the results were in, I opened the teacher's notebook when she was out of the room. My grade was higher than Shakespeare and lower than Einstein, who was then the standard. Although I knew at best that I was no genius, at last I had something of my own and I was afloat with happiness for a few hours. Shakespeare had his vocabulary and Einstein his intelligence and I, a bit of both, or a *bissel schnapps*, as the Jews say.

In fact, as with everything you feel secure about, I knew very well the limits of my own mind and that there was a ceiling to my intelligence which was, simply, good enough to do whatever I needed of it. And all my life, my mind has been a kind of staff: it has never let me down and I have always been able to lean on it. (That is what the Greeks meant by "Know thyself." Know your limits. But they meant it in a creative sense.)

So I was afloat with bonheur; at last I had something of my

own. However, without telling me, my mother telephoned the principal and asked to have me retested and he (I pieced together later) did not have the courage to refuse her and besides, what would he do if he really had a genius on his hands? Special arrangements which would have taxed his imagination, if not his kindness, would have had to be made.

So one day when I was covered with flour and sugar during cooking class, a monitor came to get me, saying that I was to be retested. "Retested?" I said, as I had a premonition of something horrible. "Yes, your mother telephoned the principal. She wants you retested."

From that point until three hours later when I left the room for delinquent children in which I was put to take the test, I was hysterical. The teacher told me, "time was up," an hour too soon. The other children yelled and screamed and snatched the examination from me since I was the only one taking a test, and I was not given any scrap paper on which to calculate. When the teacher told me that "time was up" for the second time, and I still had pages to go, I felt the way you do before you are going to be murdered. I told her, trembling, that I had a lot undone. Then she looked at her watch and said she had made a mistake, I still had half-an-hour.

I somehow got through the test and went home at three o'clock and collapsed on our green, mealy couch in the living room. "My God," I thought, "the one thing I have they won't let me keep." And I hated my mother, who only said, "Well, I wanted to be sure," getting the "w" all wrong so that it came out "Vel," with cold passion, and swore she would no longer have a daughter.

I cried hysterically on our green, living-room couch until late at night when I went upstairs to my bedroom, exhausted and convinced that I had been betrayed. As my father passed me by, he looked at me with an internal shaking of the head and clacking of the teeth, as if to say, "There she goes again. She's lost some of her marbles. What's the matter with you? All that for one test? Don't you know that you never get what you want in life, and besides, you're a simple, working man's daughter. So wake up."

My father was unaware of what had happened. My mother

61

had telephoned the school while he was at work, and he would not have understood, anyway. He only continued to stare at me silently, and then went down into the basement to all his tools, to work until midnight. There was a thick layer of life in me which he admired, but which was also his enemy.

Later the two balls of yellow leaned over me, commiserating at the second score, which was twenty points lower than the first. "You are a very intelligent girl," he said, "but you are no genius. If you were, we would have had to create a special program for you. But as it is, you can go along with the others and continue to do what you have been doing." Mr. Rowen made a slight movement toward me to indicate that he understood my loneliness, but I thought he was relieved because the mediocre order of his universe was intact.

"Raise your pencils, girls—begin," I heard, as I forgot about Mr. Rowen and the old French hag, and felt only the urge to conquer. I worked quickly, trying always to guess what answer they wanted, and I soon heard sobs on my left. I looked up and saw an amorphous, fat girl in a white, starched blouse which her mother had probably cleaned for the occasion, crying uncontrollably as she raised her mechanical pencil in the air, and then put in on her desk. "I can't go on. I can't. I'm lost," she said. The test was timed, and there was no hope for her.

Two hours later, when it was over, I saw her large bulk quivering like bags of water on the stairway, in front of an iron landing with a protective grill. I felt sorry for her, as I saw her tears still falling on the white blouse her mother had starched so carefully. I wondered, vaguely, what they were doing to us.

Several weeks later, Mr. Rowen held a slip with my acceptance in his equally yellowish hands. "Congratulations," he said. "You did it. Now I can say that someone from my school was admitted." For a moment those discolored eyes glowed with the remnant of his used idealism, which soon dimmed, and settled into his habitual look of worn, bureaucratic anxiety. I was very happy I had won and I was going into a new world, but I wondered how the blood could flow through so much yellow.

12

One day as I stood in front of the little green-stucco alcove in my bedroom in front of which I made all my private investigations, I discovered two drops of blood in my elephantine blue, nylon underpants. So I called my mother and told her I was constipated, showing her the spots as evidence, since I had read about that in the encyclopedia—where I also discovered how children are born by looking under "birth," and then went directly home and announced at the dinner table, "I found out today how children are born. The man sticks his . . ." at which point my father had an unmentionable look on his face, as if his pants had fallen down, similar to when a love scene appeared on the television. In any case, I said I was sure it was constipation, since the encyclopedia said that could produce internal bleeding. I held up my pants again as proof of my explanation. My mother said nothing. She clacked her teeth with a repetitive noise I disliked. It was a sound peculiar to people who have unhealthy teeth, which comes from a combination of fillings and bridges and unattractive, aging, bodily juices. Then she pointed her nose in the air, which meant she had special information I was too stupid to know about and which she would only reveal reluctantly—sideways, so to speak—and she said it was something else. As she left the bedroom, I screamed after her, into the hallway, that I was sure I was constipated.

Then I thought for a moment and remembered a few

months before. One afternoon when I came home from school, a friend was waiting for me on our living-room sofa, puffed up and running over with a secret. Her left eye went persistently in the wrong direction and flew to the upper left corner of the room, irrespective of the needs of the right one. As she looked at me intently with her one functioning eye, there was an unusual, lady-like expression of pride on her bloated, unsure features, and I knew in advance I was going to be jealous. I thought her father, who had much more money than mine, had bought her something. But I was wrong.

"I didn't go to school today," she said, playing with the little gold valentine on a gold string, which hung around her thick neck with its flabby creases. "Why?" I asked, feeling jealous already. "I got my period, and it hurts." Here she swelled up again and crossed her hands in her lap, like a sausage that is about to burst from its own water and fat.

"Period," came out awfully snarled and nasal, like, "pee-wee-od," as if the bad eye had got hold of it. But my friend had stepped into the promised land of breasts and a womanly something I did not have.

As she sat on her enormously rotund rear and I waited for a "pop," she rubbed her stomach with her hand to indicate that she had a unique kind of pain, although she didn't look at all sick, and then played with the absurdly small chain around her neck. By this time I was totally jealous and just glared at her. However, she had an expression of peace and happiness on her plain, bloated features which were generally nervous and insecure, which was more important to her than all my I.Q. tests and rages, and which reminded me, as I saw her continue to rub her stomach as the bad eye flew to the ceiling and she pulled at her chain, of women, when for the first time, they put their hands over their stomachs and feel a baby kicking inside. In the midst of no-matter-how-much turbulence, there is a slight pause.

I sat on my bed facing the alcove, and although I had no natural understanding of these cycles, and no pain whatsoever, I remembered my friend and realized what had happened.

13

Each morning as I passed by our thermostat, which was well below sixty, I imagined pennies dropping like malignant icicles into my parents' bank account or funeral account. The house was dead-cold and dark, as I got up before six o'clock in order to get to Hunter before eight and so deprive the late monitor of her principal pleasure in life, which was to bring me for detention to the assistant principal. I never deliberately broke the rules; they all seemed to break of their own accord, as if they had a contrary will of their own. Then I put on my grey winter coat with its silly Spanish ruff, and wrapping a wool scarf which was also a "schmatte," and handed down to me from God-knows-whom, around my neck and then over my nose and mouth so that only my eyes were exposed, I went out into the grey, unlit morning, to a decrepit gas station where I waited for the bus. This was the spine of winter, when only the promise of warmth and communal thawing got you from one place to another.

Life, or combat, began at 169 Street where I took the subway. Retrospectively, it was like a grey, mute transit system in hell, with its dirt and vomit and advertisements that promised an oral compensation for all your deficiencies. In any case, there was usually a clear, repetitive path of those who were making their way toward you, and this group of "miserables" I called the "pervert track."

The trouble was that I felt sorry for these men, in their

hodge-podge collection of grey rags, and belts that flapped around their waists, and bleary, inhuman eyes. On the other hand, you could not ignore them or you would soon feel as if you were being bitten by a fly in all sorts of places. And you could not call the police, who looked like bandits themselves, because they would only mistreat the poor pervert or put him in jail, and since I always asked myself if such-and-such-a-wretch didn't have a mother, and if so, what happened . . . I never managed to call the police. Instead, as I chewed gum vigorously and clacked my teeth against the resistant rubber in my mouth, I thought, "Yes, hell is justly administered down here." Since there was a regular route of these perverts, after a while they knew you meant business and contented themselves with glaring at you in a hideous, maniacal way.

Two hours later, I arrived at Hunter.

There was the invariable winter sky, like grey newspaper-print, which you only find in New York City and which, when you're happy, has the promise of everything. I only saw it for a minute, before I entered the cement high school with its iron door that clanged like a prison behind you, and I would not see it again until the next morning, in the few seconds between the subway and the door because by the time I got home, it was already dark. I never missed the day light, which could not penetrate Hunter's iron-barred windows, but from time-to-time it occurred to me that I never saw it. Life is divided into two parts in New York City. One for the rich who travel above ground and the other for the poor, who go underground in winter.

Our Assistant Principal, in whose office I was deposited whenever I was late, was a bird-like old maid with a layer of fluff for hair on her tidy head. She was someone who, like Aunt Sara, had always been their present age or rather, the age when she was afraid you would disrupt something or say something you oughtn't. Once you appeased that fear by sitting like a lady or by some other show of potential gentility—when in short, you did not violate any rule of good taste by referring to certain, unmentionable departments of existence—she was very kind in a quiet, resigned way, like a little bird who knows it will never fly but won't really mind if you do, so long as you are polite about it.

66

As often with women of her type, who make their lives the memento of one loss and live it out indefinitely, she had been about to marry someone who had run off and left her at the last minute. Then she had retreated forever into the peaceful, bureaucratic confines of her wood office. I eventually felt a sad depth in her passive life, which was a daily souvenir of her loss. From constantly thinking about the same thing, her face had acquired a cameo-like expression which you only noticed when you knew her. At first it was all fluff. Although I admired the constancy of her feelings, which were so unlike mine and which could make a life out of a single betrayal, I was always afraid of her and uncomfortable if she was in the room. No sooner did she appear than I felt I had done something wrong. My existence itself was a "faux pas." During the four years I knew her, I never expressed the slightest sympathy or understanding for her—not even when, finally understanding that my rebelliousness masked other qualities, she protected me from her own administrators. Any expression of feeling would have been in poor taste.

MISS X

Miss X walked into speech class—where you were forced to go even if you wanted to hang onto your subway English with all your might—with her vigorous, mannish step, like a piece of crisp celery. Balancing herself with one bony hip on her desk, she placed a neat, black leather attaché case beside her. On her skinny fingers was always a wine-dark garnet ring in a high, antique gold setting to which she added, from time-to-time, an old-fashioned bracelet studded with chiseled garnets, like cells in a bee-hive, secured with a gold safety chain. For hours I stared at these jewels, which I thought were from another world, as we discussed our "i"s and "a"s, and I fought back relentlessly by raising my hand and saying, while I wheezed my "d"s and "t"s through my nose until they broke against the window pane, "Miss X. I resent this. You are identifying education with class." Resent sounded like "wheezend" and came out awfully twisted, as if someone had got hold of the vowels and ground them into the dirt with their boots, but from then on we became great friends. In the end, Miss X got me and I soon sounded like all the other Hunter girls—in other words, like a nervous, cultivated girl from a good family.

My new accent was a curse to my father who repeated constantly, "They're ruining her. They're making her a snob. I knew I shouldn't have let her go." As for my mother, she was generally unintelligible with her private compound of English and German words, to anyone but me who knew in advance what she was going to say.

All in all, it was her jewels that occupied me for hours and represented Miss X's mysterious, coal-like interior. She had short hair and a terrible nose, a beak, in fact, such that anyone with it would have considerable difficulty adjusting to the fact. By contrast, however, her large eyes were wonderfully intelligent and alert, like a cross between a deer and a parrot. At first I thought, "Oh dear, how does she get along with that nose?" But soon I noticed only her eyes and her intelligence which went directly to the heart of a matter, or of so-and-so's motives. Her intelligence was not of the type that could make fine distinctions or bat the air in circles; it was the kind that could quickly analyze the drift or quality of a situation and reveal itself in a sentence or two, such as, "I asked you what you were thinking about and I knew you lied to me." Then you realized that she didn't mind the fact that you were lying because she knew you couldn't tell the truth. Her difficulty was that she had suspended all lyricism and compassion to a remote part of her existence, from which it only emerged occasionally when she would say, "Listen, girls, 'Tomorrow and tomorrow and tomorrow creeps . . .' isn't that perfect, lyrical?" Or when, from time-to-time, she would open her deer-like eyes in a frightened way and I had the feeling that like all of us, she was human and vulnerable. At such times her expression seemed to say, "Stay away. Don't mention anything personal to me. I can't stand it."

Her second specialty was to produce Broadway flops of which she had already directed several. Everything was a sales item to Miss X, despite her classical education and keen mind. Even Shakespeare was a successful maker of plays, they sold well and pleased everybody. Besides, most of life was wrapping.

When I told her about my family, still wheezing my d's and

t's, and getting the "a" all wrong so that it sounded as if it had crawled out from an underground tunnel, she maintained a cold, sympathetic distance, the same distance she had from all human sweat and pain. She only said that I should be careful to make sure that my father did not injure me permanently because in that case, the law could interfere. I felt that she understood me by the contrast between our two natures, but that her internal promise not to suffer had created something brittle and nervous in her.

I always picture her exactly as she was and think that no clusters of veins, or white hair, will seriously affect her energy.

She was like a kind, efficient machine that had got going, and would continue running backwards and forwards without change until it collapsed in a heap of its own metal parts and screws. Tolstoy would have said that she was like a tree that never bore fruit, but I don't agree. I think she was true to herself, but constructed with a loss.

There was a secret in her life which she would take to the grave with her, perhaps in her early family, or perhaps it was the beak. And so it is that the best people, because of one particular fear live through their students, remote from experience themselves, like puppets in the snow.

14

Aristotle was right, learning begins with wonder and my intelligence and memory were drowned in the expectation of these nightly battles.

These scenes usually began at dinner, when we were all seated around a wood table in the little, green, Spanish-style room next to the kitchen. My father's presence itself had become intolerable to me, like a suffocating odor. So one evening, I deliberately pushed my chair as far away from him as possible so that I would be out of his reach, but also because I knew this would provoke him. Something drove me to continuously manifest the repulsion I felt for him. Then he asked me a trivial question and I replied in a peevish, barely audible way without looking at him and the cycle was under way.

This was all the excuse he needed. By the next minute his features had snarled into a malevolent hiss and his nose seemed to spread and become disproportionately large, so that it took over his face which he put close to mine. I was forced to remain in that position, from where I could feel his breath and see the deformed spread of his nostrils. It was this moment—of being forced to remain near him as I waited for him to attack— that did me as much harm as any beating itself. In any case, he said, "Say Father." "Yes." "Yes, what?" "Yes." "I'll teach you to be disrespectful, you little brat. With all your grand ideas. Get off your chair and go to the living room." I had to walk to my own execution.

Then he took off his old-fashioned wristwatch with the gold and pink case and delicate black numbers, and put it carefully on the bannister. This remnant of reason, which also prevented him from leaving marks on me or doing anything he could be punished for, increased my feeling of horror, as if the murderer was grooming and pomading himself, calculating how long it would take him to finish off his victim before he began. This ounce of self-control only emphasized his power, as if the watch were worth more than I. There was, however, one proviso: whereas the murderer wants his victim dead, my father needed me alive so he could return for more.

Then he threw me on the floor in front of the hand-perforated speakers in the sound system he had built, dragged me around by my hair, and then kicked my back, as he said, "I'll teach you to obey. You have to learn to be a woman. Hunter is ruining you."

My mother stood by screaming uselessly, in a vague way that was directed at the windows and doors and not at all at my father, as she threatened to call the police which she never did. Her screaming was like a beater during a hunt, who secretly encouraged the hunter by arousing him still more and further terrifying the animal. I felt that my mother encouraged my father because I was still the object of his attention, no matter what form it took. There was a look of collateral lust, or collateral vengeance on their faces, for which I have never forgiven her. I thought that she was secretly glad that my father was beating me because she hoped that in this way, he would destroy me, just as she herself had been destroyed. In the six years during which these chronic attacks occurred, she never made the slightest attempt to protect me. It is this, when I am inclined to be lenient and understanding to my mother, which is most difficult . . .

My sister was silent and frightened. Her unsure expression, with its permanent freckles and light-brown, curly hair, seemed to say, "Look what a mess you've made for yourself and now no one can do anything. Why don't you just keep quiet, like me?"

She was the only one who was genuinely sorry I was being beaten, but her punishment was worse than mine. My father ignored her, he hardly spoke to her and took no interest in what she did at school. She was like a little sunflower with freckles all over for seeds, that never got enough light or water and which, if you pushed it a little further, would stop growing altogether. She had a frightening way of opening her eyes wide and staring at nothing, at which point you felt some manic vacuity in her and clacked your teeth to yourself and forgot momentarily about your own problems, as you thought, "The poor kid."

Then, just as the murderer sees that his victim is lifeless and his fury diminishes, so too, the look of lust and rage on my father's face was replaced by a malevolent hiss. And just as the murderer takes a final look to make sure his victim is really dead, he kicked me once or twice more and then went down into the basement saying, "This too will pass. I have to teach you."

Men such as my father, whose outlook is simple and who cannot, as a result, understand why life bears no resemblance to their dreams of work and marriage and in general, the rewards of a serious attitude which allows only momentary pleasure and whose rule is work, such men often have closed circuits in their minds and live in a private world where they are the victims of cruel, manipulative forces. He felt that Hunter and my defiant character were his enemies, since my later role in life was to be submissive. And he had identified my later role, which was the underside of all he respected, with my relationship to him. In short, he treated me like an unfaithful mistress whose betrayal consisted of my wanting to breathe freely in my own particular way. It is for this reason that I often watch the birds when I see them flying freely near the sun and clouds. Without exaggeration and in spite of the self-indulgence which these likenesses encourage, I envy the birds and sometimes think that it is because I am a woman that I cannot be like them.

At first the murderer needed to be right and explain that he was only trying to inculcate sane principles, which meant doing what he said, but later on he stopped justifying himself at all.

Soon an insane niche which required these beatings for release—which came from the distance between my father's

72

treatment of me and the fact that he knew, at bottom, that I was his daughter—developed in his mind, just as when you first smoke a cigarette, you don't like the taste and you wonder why you are doing this. Then you try another and soon you are so addicted that you cannot exist for three hours without running out to get a pack. On the other hand, I felt that he never lost his edge of self-control and that having the option of restraint, he chose not to exercise it. But who knows if the murderer, when he prepares and nourishes his victim in advance and plants a hatchet or gun, could really do otherwise.

One New Year's Eve, my father came to the entry door in our hallway as I was about to leave with a friend, and leaning forward in his thick, increasingly sluggish way, warned me to be home by midnight, finishing with an ominous "otherwise." In the way children have of accepting the most grotesque situations, my friend, who was an intelligent boy and interested in the sciences, made a mental click to the effect that here the Gladstones were at it again. By then the beatings were an established fact and we had a long way to go by subway, in the cold, so that everyone knew it was impossible for me to be back by midnight. In order for me to return on time, I would have had never to leave at all. My father added, "If you're one minute late, I'll give it to you." Nature had by then caught up with herself and compensated for being so slow, by doubling all her activities with the result that my figure was round and fully mature at fourteen. Then my father repeated, "Remember what I said . . . I'll give it to you."

When I returned, it was a quarter past twelve. I went in quickly through the entrance hall with its boots and umbrellas and into the living room, where an enraged bulk, whose heaviness jolted out of the chair as if it had been waiting for hours for this moment, grabbed me by the neck and started to squeeze. His eyes were emitting flashes from the other side of his mind and this time, I knew it was going to be bad.

"I'll teach you," he said, although he seemed to have no idea of what, exactly, he was trying to teach me. Then he added, as if he had found the crux of his idea, "To disobey."

Then he tightened his hold on my neck and squeezed the

veins until by the pressure, I almost thought he was going to strangle me, but even then, I knew he needed me alive. He continued to squeeze and kick me, gradually releasing the pressure on my neck, until finally he let me go.

This time I was genuinely hysterical and swore to myself, in my bedroom, that I would leave my house and go somewhere else to live. I considered making myself a ward of the state, but then I remembered what my father had told me about the orphanage and what I had read in Dickens, and pictured to myself daily portions of oatmeal in long, filthy rooms with rows of benches, and decided that might be worse.

It was two years before I managed to leave, but when I am not angry and am in the mood to be forgiving, I think of how my father must have sat alone on our dreary couch in the living room on New Year's Eve as he waited for the one thing he had loved, and which had left him, to return; how he must have thought that his life was in ruins and that he had worked so hard all those years for nothing. I ask myself, when I feel a soft pliant "oh," in what he could have found comfort, in what early memories of warmth or maternal care, but he was an orphan and his mother had been too poor to take care of him, so he must have raged and beat me in a pocket of the most total isolation and natal despair.

15

Two years passed. My father found a job in another state and moved into a solitary, cheerless apartment with imitation wood-panelled walls. It was the type of gloomy thoughtless place bachelors choose when they are in a hurry, and don't really expect anything good to happen. He returned to Queens for the weekend, late on Friday night, when he released whatever he had been accumulating during the week in incessant beatings.

This was the worst period for him. He rarely spoke except to give commands such as "Sit up, keep quiet, say 'Father' when you speak to me." And all these imperatives were the pretext for a fresh attack, since they were never properly obeyed. He was like a man eaten by a disease which has the characteristic not only of destroying its own organism, but everything else it touches.

His features separated still more, and acquired an unhealthy expression, like a snarl, which I associated with self-repulsion. There were always bits of white mucous in the corners of his eyes, which reenforced the impression that he had a disease or a hereditary misfunction. In any case, partly from middle age and partly from the habit of snarling, he acquired a stiff, corpse-like way of walking as if the middle of him, which was getting thick, moved with difficulty and the rest, since it was attached, followed against its will.

There was something missing in his expression, as if a vacuity had replaced life, which said, "Don't bother me. It's safer to hate everything, since that is the accurate state of affairs anyway. And don't think you can pull anything over me because I'm prepared, and I know I don't stink no worse." He looked in fact, as if he were always smelling something foul. He continued in that state for the next two years.

In the beginning of August, when the Catskill mountains spread like lumps of dough on a housewife's board over the sleeping countryside, a slender, over-dressed man of medium height sat down next to me on a bench. His crooked face, which pulled away from the fulcrum as if a negative force had gotten hold of it and wrenched it from its proper foundation, had an air of subterranean doing which he did not want to understand. He wore an alligator belt and silk-blend trousers, while all of nature cried out for largess and the absence of calculation. I realized that he had become a machine attached to his pale demiworld. Then he asked me in a nasal, New York City accent which slid out sideways from his uneven lips, "Are you my daughter's counselor? It's nice of you to take so much time with her."

His mouth parted and one side drooped as he spoke quietly, in the twittering pa-ta-tee that characterizes people when they meet and are attracted. As he continued, the rolling, memoryless landscape surrounded us with all the elements of a medieval countryside in which little farmers and peasant women in their rags and multiple scarves and codpieces sleep, or eat, or lie drunk, around a wine keg. He told me about his life and business and all his money, as the dark material slid to the other end of the fulcrum where it gathered negative momentum and the incapacity to generate life or hope or anything except more of itself. There was an odd vacuity in his face, which would have been handsome because of the green-brown eyes and black, semitic hair, if it had been even.

"So you want to learn about life?" he asked me half-an-hour later, as if that too could fit into a scientist's neat category. "Well, I think that's very nice." At this point Joseph, for that was the stranger's name, turned away so that his profile was momentarily etched against the waving, dessicated landscape.

He seemed to be considering something which hung in a doubtful balance so that the light in his face, which was always a glimmer and more absent than present, gleamed as if to taper and then turning into a naught, vanished altogether.

"It doesn't exist," he said, replying to what I meant. "It's a chimera, like a four-sided triangle." Then, as the uncertain material slipped and slid to the other notch of his character and all the underground elements gathered momentum and an incandescent, eerie animus from which life and the expectation of pleasure were absent; at this point, when the grey flu of his smoky soul was in place, it concentrated, held, and then spiraled out in a series of convulsions that jarred the irregular topography of his crooked face.

I knew then that this stranger to whom I was so drawn, although I immediately understood the prostitutes and hundreds of women who would fill what could not exist, was seriously deformed and that his unhappy life had been accompanied by all his tics and contortions so that there was a hopeless, quiet counterpoint from which he could never escape.

"Just stay young and beautiful," he added when everything was still again, "The rest is decoration."

"But I want you to love me," I replied, hitching up the top of my black bathing suit which was supposed to make me look like an Italian actress. It was of the old-fashioned type and made of many bones which pinched me but had magazine allure.

This time there was no wavering or transit of the uncertain material, if a vacuity can be called a thing. Instead he looked at me principally through his one good eye and shook his head.

"What are your plans?"

"I'm still in high school."

"Oh, I can see you are a very intelligent girl, but what do you like to do?"

"I've never known a man."

"How old are you?"

"Sixteen . . . but I'm mature for my age."

"Yes, I can see that." He laughed as the uneven side of his face hung from a crooked hanger and then fell off altogether.

As we began to talk and I estimated quickly, through some internal form of calculation of whose mechanism I was unaware,

what was going to happen; as the uncomputerized sun continued to shine down on this man's face which was already dear and
deformed, I thought of a scene from Breughal which was either
real or imagined. At the end of summer when the hay was cut
and the brown earth dessicated from the long months, the peasants put down their sickles and rakes and the women their various utensils and everyone lay down under the shade of his
twisted trees. Wine urns lay nearby, and wooden plates, and
there was the primitive gathering of their medieval rags and
aprons as everything was momentary peace and the absence of
midday motion. Into this air of held stillness Joseph, with all his
worries and deep fear, as deep as the sun and as long as time,
which attracted me to him although I understood its boundary
and content; all this, like the hay and reposing peasants, led to a
form of elusive, heavy peace in which the myriad, hot elements
were held and contained by the warm, passionate artist.

"Will I see you in the city?" I asked, feeling sure that I would.

"Yes, of course. You are such a sweet girl."

There was no longer any conflict or hesitation of the underworld material, it was all resolved in a black plateau from which
light or self-questioning was prohibited. Then as Joseph told
me about his factories and money—he had apparently invented something and become quite rich, or at least made the
million dollars which satisfied his criteria—the incandescent,
neon quality returned like an old friend whose tics and addic-
tion you welcome because that's the way it is.

"I'm going to go in," he said, as the same absence slithered
back and forth and then pinged around in its circumscribed
orbit. "I think I'll take a nap after lunch."

As I looked at the lean definition of a man in his late thirties
which was so different than mine, I imagined Joseph in a way
that became permanently attached to him so that whenever I
thought of him, I thought of this. I imagined a lonely soldier
going into combat with the expectation of neither victory nor
defeat, but only of continued, isolated battle. And the paces and
the terrain were somewhere in the sky, so that this poor warrior
walked on steps made of time, not space. And so up and up.
Alone, defeated, wealthy and whoring, like a poor soldier who
has never had a chance and only knows how to fight.

16

In October, when the leaves fall in New York City like the grey punctuation in a young artist's manuscript as they momentarily rival the dirt, and roaches, and multiplying crime—when humanity bows to the needs of the incumbent autumn so that we begin to put on hats and jackets and the tweedy paraphernalia that mark the change in that season—Joseph rented a room in a small, ordinary hotel. I wore a raincoat with a fake black lining and a black hat, which from prostration, was entitled to entry in my mother's schmatte collection. It was perched over one eye at what I thought was a seductive angle. He wore his invariable blue and white pin-striped suit and all the clutter of the perfectly matching, alligator accessories. We were like two people hollering across a drawbridge who hoped it would remain down long enough for them to talk for a while.

The room itself was oblong with a bed and nightstand at one corner and a window covered by a beige venetian blind at the other. It belonged to a chain of similar hotels. Joseph was calm; the complicated gear of his jarred nature was momentarily absent as he caught an élan I had never seen before and then held onto it with a bizarre momentum that came from a place I did and did not possess and which it would have frightened me to understand.

As the same momentum continued, with the reassuring rhythm of the leaves as they fell in myriad colors on the pavement and garbage pails, he put his arm around me. He seemed, from an inner question mark, to be considering some matter with which I was not to interfere. Then sliding back and forth in it, he left it unresolved and said, "Don't worry, Anne. It only takes a few minutes and it won't hurt. Then later on we can talk."

"I'm not scared," I replied, although I was. This was the big event, after all, and the one I had been plotting with such a variety of mishaps as I went to sleep next to the wall or fought with all the forces that threatened what I wanted in the form of Mother, or Father, or general metropolitan villany.

Then there was sharp, piercing pain, like little pincers, which excluded anything else and prevented me from catching the same feeling or anything at all resembling pleasure. When I looked up, instead of the usual orchestra of tics and droning, irregular mechanisms, he was different. It was as if this bizarre force which I had glimpsed momentarily on my father's misanthropic face, or seen in animals, had gotten hold of his expressionless, triste soul and deformed it into its own image, like the creation in reverse. He looked, in short, like cats or dogs or other wild animals who leave their homes at night and bat their mindless brains at the empty moon. Thus he prowled around in search of some lunar objective which it would not have satisfied him to have. And, like these pets, he grasped and searched for something that was either very deep inside, or else very far outside himself; but in any case, impossible to obtain.

As he continued his eerie search which I could tell by the moonish disproportion in his unhappy eyes he would never stop, I tried not to cry. I remembered, instead, the bums and beggars and all the garbage people that line the New York City streets like a living momento mori. The plethora of ambulatory inexistence and the strange carving of man's imagination from nothing, came to me together with the simple advice, "Wait for him and be patient."

Soon his expression changed and instead of the wild beast, something open and gentle, like an orchid, appeared. This was the closest thing to peace I ever saw. Then the piercing pains ceased and I cried a little.

"You were such a brave girl," he said.

"It hurt," I replied. Then he laid his head on my chest where there are the little, chicken-like bones and as I felt its sad warmth, I thought of the lonely soldier who puts down his arms with the knowledge that this is only a deceptive pause and that soon he will have to pick them up again. "You are such a sweet girl," he repeated in the tone of paternal approbation he always adopted when talking to me. "Really, with a lot of guts."

"But I want you to love me."

"I'm telling you Anne," he said, pushing the ambiguous material to the other side of the fulcrum so that a slight tremor replaced the former smoothness of his ruffled features, "it doesn't exist. It's like a four-sided triangle."

Then, from the apparent pause in any normal feeling, it was obvious that Joseph was having another series of tics and convulsions as he remembered something painful. "What do you know?" he asked with his sideways air of muffled pathos when the cross of his face had settled. "You're so beautiful and desirable."

"What is it?"

"Well," he said, in the same subway voice that was running over with New York City perverts and whole layers of underworld doing, "I always wanted to die as a kid. I walked around ashamed of the head on my shoulders and knowing that the bottom was even worse."

"What did you just remember?"

"As a child I had a series of painful operations. I got an infection, nowadays it would be nothing. Just a little anaesthesia and it's finished, but that was before the days of modern antibiotics and the surgeon who operated, I don't know if he was drunk or just incompetent, in any case he slipped and cut a critical nerve. Then my whole face sagged."

"I love you," I repeated. "I don't care."

"Leave me alone for a while, Anne," he said. Then I opened the venetian blind and looked out of the window next to our bed. Under the network of New York City lights, the streets and pavement moved with life and seemed to sway back and forth from their own momentum, like a children's carousel. Up and down, back and forth went the tremulous activity of the weird night and only silence was asleep. Over and below the lighted rocking horses and other toys, the leaves fell and gathered late into the night, making an inaudible patter of hope.

As I looked back at this man who was sunk in the paraphernalia of his own, unhappy past, I decided to leave him alone and instead pushed one of the blinds so that I could see outside. Then, for the first time, as one element was passive and the other filled with active, rhythmic creation which was the proliferation of itself, I felt a universal "ah." "Yes," I thought as a sweet flu of order spread over the whole thing, "It all makes sense. My mother's camps, my father's beatings, my other world." Without looking back, I knew that Joseph would not have moved or altered the morbid turgidity of his purblind soul and I felt what I called to myself "an expansion of consciousness." It always came to me in just those terms and was always repeated when Joseph, like my father, was busy with something else.

A short while later—when whatever pause or dark material had been resolved into itself so that the slight reciprocal space between us, did and did not exist, like a joint chimera—Joseph turned on the light on the old, wood nightstand beside the bed and reached for the college applications I had left there. Then for the next half hour, he dictated a scientist's biography and aspirations, or in short, his own.

"It doesn't sound like me," I remarked, as I listened to the dry vita.

"Just do it, Anne," he said, "and be a good girl."

"What do you think will happen?" I asked later, when the applications were completed and lying in a heap on the nighttable near my raincoat and hat.

"Happen," he repeated, as if the question had arrived from nowhere and had no relevance to me, him, or whatever incipient fulcrum there was between us. Then Joseph searched for a category in which to put this, or any question, and he replied as he always did by referring it to something he was already sure about, so that it slipped, to use a mathematician's language, into a blank set which was for him, universal.

"Why nothing ever happens," he answered, as he grabbed the area of the set and placed this new article in it. "Whatever

82

do you mean?" Then this particular unit acquired a periphery of others, so that it was bordered by similar, repressive material. Feeling comforted by the galaxy of negation around him and reaching into the slight black material it contained, he said, "There's neat, clean work and intelligent fun."

"Nothing else?"

Joseph did not answer. The simple question sank, deepened and churned around in a dark well from which it did not escape. As it stayed there, other realms, whole constellations of mirth and philosophy flew ambiguously over the same terrain. He remained motionless and did not reply or look at me or give any sign of life. For the first time I saw, apart from myself or my own needs, what lay at the bottom of the entire edifice, like a lost scream among the myriad New York City tenements. It was not anger or fear, but the simple despair of the lost soldier who has only had a short reprieve and has just been reminded that he will have to fight again. The pitiful scream widened, deepened and found its passive form as, without moving, Joseph opened his one good eye. To answer, there were a hideous series of tics and contortions and I turned away, involuntarily, as you do when you are ashamed. Through the venetian blind, there was the endless pitter-patter of multicolored leaves which fell inaudibly on the grey cement below.

17

One Sunday afternoon when I was reading upstairs in my bedroom, my father asked me to come to the living room, saying we had something important to discuss. When I got to the bottom of the spiral-shaped, wood bannister, I saw my mother sitting beside my sister on our shabby, green couch, in front of which there was a black and white coffee table. That inexpensive wood coffee table had always represented luxury to me, although it was very ordinary. Perhaps because it was made of real wood and varnished. There was an unusual glitter in my mother's small, shrewd eyes, like glass that is momentarily animate, but underneath there was something persistently cold and alien. My sister looked frightened, as she usually did and as if she expected a catastrophe and only hoped to escape before it struck. My father was considerate and even polite, which made me suspect a trick.

"Sit down, Anne," he said in mellifluous, unnatural tones. "Your mother and I have something important to discuss with you girls. We have reached a decision and have decided to try to live together again. I will move back next Friday. Well, how do you feel about it?"

I quickly reasoned in the following way. My father probably had a new job near us which made it convenient to live at home. On the other hand, if he moved back, it would be impossible for me to see Joseph, since I often returned well after midnight. Furthermore, I could see by the weak, helpless look on my mother's face that she believed everything would be good and different in the future. "Can you patch up hatred?" I asked myself. "How can she be so blind?" but I said nothing. There was a clear threat in my father's soft, conciliatory voice which was naturally deep, as if he had already assumed the feudal, proprietary rights that living at home would reestablish.

"Well, Anne, what do you have to say?"

"I don't believe it. It won't work. After a few days everything will be the same," I replied.

A frown that reminded me of Zeus, when Homer says an olympian shadow like a mountain darkens his face, contracted my father's features. He raised his arm to hit me and I was forced to look at the individual, thick fingers, like fat cigars, through which the blood had stopped flowing normally, as if his circulation had joined his soul as both refused to work properly. Then he decided to control himself and lowered his arm, which shook from repressed rage. My father's expression, as he looked at me, was never normal but driven by the urge to destroy my privacy. It was a mixture of lust and wrath. That moment of rational hesitation convinced me that there was a financial reason for his returning.

"You brat," he said, "I knew you would try to ruin things. Well, your mother and I have decided and I'm coming back next Friday and no miserable, arrogant, pessimistic little . . . . who thinks she's better than everyone else because she goes to a fancy school where they give you airs. Never mind, I'll teach you."

We were like a Homeric caucus of the gods, where each one sits and schemes in his own interest and the result is war.

So I made an instant decision. I would leave. Long ago, when I was a little girl and I heard those nocturnal stories about Hitler, I decided that if he ever reappeared or anyone like him, I would pack up my things and run. I wouldn't ask questions or wait to verify his doings. If I had children, I would take them with me, under my arm if necessary. This is part of what I call "The Pogrom Mentality."

However, in order to escape successfully, I had to make my plans and say nothing. I calculated that if I bought only food and subway tokens, I could live on the twelve to fifteen dollars a week my mother gave me. I loved mushrooms, which were then only thirty-five cents a pound, and I could have them every day for dinner cooked in butter and spices. There was always an empty, single bed in the basement of Sara and Michael's home, next to the boiler room. I knew they didn't like me, but there is a family instinct among Jews; they will criticize you night and day but they won't leave you in the streets.

Then I thought of one major obstacle. I imagined Michael screaming at the top of the stairs, while his bad eye trembled like lightning in its socket and his voice rose to a falsetto which rattled the piano-like bones in his chest, "Turn off the light. Only one light at a time. The electricity bill is terrible." Then I thought of Joseph in his lean, businessman's suit and the slight "thump" from his lips, and then of my father's raised, trembling hand and I never hesitated again. It was simple. When my father left that evening, I would pack everything I could in advance and then come home early one afternoon from Hunter, before the winter sun set at five o'clock, and leave.

And from that time on, it has always seemed to me that the hard work of life is decided alone and in the dark, when no one is there. It's only joy and success that we share. Some people say that making a decision is really choosing between two alternatives, you do this rather than that, but that has never happened to me. (In fact, those who espouse the doctrine of "choice" must have a great deal of money, or leisure, or both.) Rather, it has always been like driving along a path that leads off a cliff. You know you have to avoid falling into the darkness and you will take any other road, no matter what it is like. The decision is to avoid the abyss, the rest is unclear.

In any case, when my father left that Sunday evening, I packed whatever would not crease into my bamboo satchel, leaving my dresses and skirts hanging in the closet. Then I opened the secretary which my father had constructed from unvarnished plywood ten years before and found a lumpy, white envelope with two wads of grey, shredded cotton and a tiny brassiere, which was also filthy, and of an indescribable color under the arms which had declined from white to a mealy greenish-black. For a moment I remembered the fear and pain associated with my first brassiere, then I threw it out. There was another envelope with the bristly stumps of two braids which my mother had cut when I was twelve. They were still sturdy and brown, and unaffected by time. I also found a leather diary I had kept briefly when I was nine. Opening it at random, I read, "Mommy screamed and nagged me all day. What a bitch. How I hate her." I had forgotten how long ago it all began and threw the diary away, making an internal vow that included happy children and unending tenderness. In fact, that is what I had always done. The more evil and nastiness I saw around me, the more I promised to be good. But there was a pocket, a gap between the two extremes, which made me wild and nervous. Then, as always before you move, I tried to imagine myself in my new home. I calculated that if I came home from Hunter late, after dinner, Sara and Michael would already be in bed since Sara had to get up, like the sun, before it was light to go to the noodle factory.

I spoke to no one except Miss X. about the change, explaining to her that my feelings for Joseph would sustain me in my new, mole-like habitat. In the mechanical, melodramatic way which was still very kind, in which I had heard her dispose of so many people, she told me to follow my passionate, difficult destiny and that the law was probably on my side. It had never occurred to me that anything I did was related to "destiny," that was a term reserved for the gods and Shakespeare's heroes. I replied that my father had a deep fear of the police, or of any external authority, and would never go to them. She said that I could always come to her if I needed anything and that I should be sure to eat well and take care of myself.

So on Wednesday afternoon I collected my bank book, alarm clock, and make-up and putting it all into my bamboo satchel, went downstairs to leave. My mother stood by passively, just as I imagine she must have watched many catastrophes, without trying to stop me. She had a frightening, stony look in her small, glittering eyes which was devoid of all humanity or laughter, like a trapped cat that slinks inward and can only think of its claws. That stony expression had increased as she sensed the approaching end of our family, which in her mind, was the same thing as the reappearance of Hitler. A fatalistic wave was beginning which, within two years, was to turn her into a half-crazy, or three-quarters crazy old lady who lived an underground existence in a low-income housing project in Queens, very much as we all had begun twenty years earlier. She didn't scream or protest, that was what was dangerous. She only said she would visit me once a week on Sunday to give me my allowance and make sure I was all right.

Seeing that frozen, helpless look and hearing her tell me to try to be nice to Sara and Michael, otherwise I would hurt their feelings—by which I was to understand that I was always hurting hers—I picked up my satchel and left.

Outside it occurred to me again that there was such a thing as a "Pogrom Mentality," by which the individual members of a nation recreate their national experience, that is what my mother had done. She had repeated the cycle that had made her leave Germany.

When I looked back, my mother was standing in the doorway crying. Her energy and motion were concentrated inward, in a spot bound and cut off from contact with anything outside herself. She wore a torn yellow sweater, a schmatte which was too small and belonged to my sister, and her plump arms hung defenselessly at her sides. The tears fell over a thick, invariable layer of cold cream which she always wore to keep her skin from drying, which gave out a distinct, slightly sweet odor.

When I left the subway, it was almost dark. A tweezer could have squeezed between day and night. I bought a pound of mushrooms at a local store and then rang Sara's doorbell. Nothing had changed. As I cooked my mushrooms, Sara served the chicken soup with noodles from her factory in the same white porcelain dishes with the little rose pattern. This was followed by the invariable, frugal portions of "fleish mit kartoffel," meat and potatoes. There was just enough to maintain them both at their constant weight. Then Michael rolled his left eye toward the stove, over which a nasty second light was burning. This was the preparation. Then his eye flew around uncontrollably in its socket while the rest of him trembled, and he screamed at Sara to turn it off. It was winter and the electricity bill was terrible. I thought that he was in a state of permanent shock from World War I. The physical injury to his eye would not account for the trembling that convulsed his body and made him almost helpless. He was a tailor and I wondered how on earth he could thread a needle with all that jerking. Then with a patient, martyred look, the story of how Michael had saved her life by taking her out of Germany occurred to me. Sara said that he shouldn't upset himself and that they had a guest. By a compensating reaction, to prove he liked what was his own, he put his arm around Sara and said, "Ja, Ja: Das ist die Sara. Yes, yes, this is Sara." Die Sara, however, did not react and with an expression that implied that she was used to his outbursts in either direction, wiped away an imaginary speck from beside her plate. Then Michael gave me a key with a knowing, slightly vulgar expression which convinced me of what I already suspected, that my mother had told them about Joseph. He said that I should be quiet and not wake them up when I came home.

They said I could stay as long as I watched the electricity and then asked me about my homework and my father. From their icy questions and their lack of affection or understanding of my life, I could see more signs of my mother's work. "She has a good brain but no heart," was evident in their attitude, which was exactly the same as my mother's. Like her, they never commented on my appearance as you usually do with a young girl, and never asked me how I felt so I was glad I had bought my own mushrooms. Momentarily, in an outburst of generosity Michael said, and I am reconstructing his words, because they came out so jerkily and mostly in German, "She was wonderful. Die Anne. The way you learned to play blocks when you were little, only four. I showed you once and you did it. She put them all together. And then we played a record in French and half-an-hour later you were still singing it. Das var wunderbar. Ya."

I took a look in their bedroom, on the other side of the kitchen through a white, wood door. There was still the miraculous picture of Sara as a young woman with her bare shoulders seductively draped in velvet. On the dresser was the same pocket edition of *Nana*, with a naked lady wrapped in a whirl of gauze on the cover, and a bottle of German cologne. "The same one," I thought.

At eight o'clock they went to bed, after Sara had done the dishes and wiped away the nonexistent dirt with rubber gloves. Her silence seemed predatory to me and like my mother, she had a stony expression in her eyes which was softened by the invariable routine of her house. I thought the women in my family all had the same thing rolling around in their heads.

Then I, too, left the kitchen. I climbed down an ordinary, dark stairway leading to the basement and when I got to the bottom, I saw a cot with a lamp and a small nighttable. About ten yards from the landing, on the other side of the bed, was a green boiler room with a furnace inside. This furnace frightened me, since it was old and a dark, moldy green, and constantly made a gurgling noise which diminished or increased depending on how much fuel was being burned. The room was like a narrow, greyish-brown box hung with cobwebs for curtains; the cobwebs, however, were imaginary, since the room itself was spotless. It was only the darkness that made it seem like an underground chamber. At the opposite end was a toilet, a bathtub, and then a door leading to the garden.

I unpacked my things and took a bath, leaving on an extra light to compensate for the basement gloom. That was a mistake. Soon I heard, "Sie ist verruckt; she is crazy." The door to the basement opened and Michael yelled down that I could only use one light at a time. I told him I couldn't turn it off because the switch was at the top of the stairs, and I would have to climb back down in the dark. "Ach, ich bin müd; oh, I'm tired," he said, and switched the light off, slammed the door, and then disappeared.

Then I crawled into bed, pulling the feather quilt they had placed on top of an army blanket over me. It seemed odd to be sleeping next to a boiler room, so I let the light on a small table beside my bed burn all night.

18

One evening when the multicolored autumn leaves had turned white so that beautiful, anxious snow fell copiously on the cement blocks below like a child's fingers or the probing movements of love; when there was an intermittent curtain of blobs of white, illuminated by halo-like rounds above the street-lights and traffic signals; and when in short, nature like white typewriter ink, erased the filth and multiplying pollution of our city and halloed out a kind, clean welcome to the dark night above, then Joseph appeared in a pin-striped suit and perfectly matching alligator accessories and we went to the anonymous hotel room.

Inside, there was a declining patchwork of beige and grey which nevertheless managed to stay neat. There was a small nightstand with a lamp at one end of the double bed and the same window with its venetian blind forming the sole aperture in this ordinary, standard room.

"Turn off the light," Joseph said as he lay down on top of the blankets in the huge bed without stirring or taking off his clothes.

"But I like the light," I replied as I nevertheless shut it off and then undressed and got under the covers between him and the nighttable. Soon, in the fan-like spread of grey, I could distinguish both Joseph and the night lamp. The room, with inverted shades of vague, dark absence, acquired more and more sombre definition and outline as my eyes adjusted to the

91

slight light which now came in through the systematic cracks in the venetian blind. Joseph lay absolutely limp and motionless and refused to speak or acknowledge the existence of anything other than some grey matter which, like our room, had seeped inside in the place where speech and life had formerly been. Out of this concavity, which had only incipient bars of theoretical light, I finally heard, "Can you beat that?"

"What?"

"What?" he repeated, laughing, so that even in the dull vacuity of our apparent, nothing-like room, I could outline the moving curvature of his bent, meaty lips, "I'm getting impotent, that's what." The grey remained very stable and formed a systematic, irregular collage of its own elements as it entered into the dim heap already in our room. Then the pieces of this shifting canvas reshuffled and out of the new formula, which only resorted its former, declining components, Joseph said, "Would you believe it? A man of thirty-two with a girl of sixteen." He always lied to me about his age.

"Turn out the light, Anne," he repeated as I tried to switch it on. "I don't want to see tonight." As he continued to lie in that mummy-like position, without hope or joy or the nascent under-pinning of returning life, I said that I didn't mind and that I was glad just to be with him. The same reluctant material then, as if it were considering and rejecting the brighter side of its own spew, slid to the left and rocked and bathed itself in the waste product of its own poisoned metabolism. "After all," he said, as like became like and he went back and forth in the same by-material, so that a cakey residue of froth collected at the unseen edges of his imagined corpus and hope, like light, flew to some far-away recess where it could no longer be seen. "I've known so many women. Can you beat that?"

"What happened?"

"You mean other than the fact that my wife humiliated me last night? Nothing. Leave me alone, Anne." Then the imaginary rows of ancient mummies, and the primitive, artisan's inner boxes that cover the dead bodies with decreasing circumference, so that all you see is the painted imitation of death; all these fitted casings seemed to peel off Joseph as he looked neither at me, nor the room, nor at anything that had any relationship to motion. At the heart of the painted mummy, with its multiple layers of rustic, geometric artifice, was the same plaintive scream that lay like a lost paralysis among the myriad tenements of the New York City night, unwitnessed except by me.

Layer after layer of identical casing fell off and I understood that I should let him be, so I looked out the window instead, through a crack in the venetian blind. There, by contrast, the same white curtain of intrepid blobs fell quietly as if to counter, by its soothing rhythm, the travail of the man inside. So white, peaceful like the promise of everything you want which lies delusively under the edge of the snowfall or at the bottom of the night.

"Come here, Anne," he finally said.

"I am here," I replied, moving closer to him, although he was still fully dressed and I quite naked.

"Just stay here." Then the dark material receded and was transformed into a writer's ink as he tries to understand and probe his breathing manuscript. Black became black as the ink flowed again to form small, hesitant letters. Joseph was apparently considering the same subject as he put his arm around me in a rare moment of tacit peace and the absence of grinding tension. He continued to hold me like a friend or sister as the indecision slid to its positive side and he said, sotto voce, while the words came out of his unlevered lips, "I would wait for you."

Had there been a myth for this relationship, as if it were a person, it would have been as follows: that it was composed of many strata. The bottom was deep and fertile and for the most part, impregnable; the middle peaceful and gentle and where the two could find momentary repose; and the top, or most apparent strata, full of treachery and deceit and the one which would undo the others by its inner conflagration.

Then in the brief blanket of the second stratum I turned on the light and Joseph had another horrible series of nervous contortions. When they subsided, he lightened the slight pressure on my shoulder so that I could feel the lean articulation of his arm beneath the business suit. He continued to resolve the same matter in this new direction and said, "It's important for you to get an education, right?"

"I want to learn," I replied, caught myself in the new material which I knew was transitory and suspended at either end by conclaves of whores and other villany.

Then this middle layer reappeared and held us two momentary figures in its delusive grasp as the lever between us altered and moved toward me. I knew that I would leave him at the end of the year when I went to college and that he would not want me to go. And as the delicate needle of the metronome went back and forth between us and fluctuated toward the new end, I looked again through the window to see the beautiful dropping snowflakes which, like the memory of love or a child's fingers, would exist forever, late and falling, long after we two were gone.

19

My regime of sauteed mushrooms and spices, cooked after Sara and Michael were in bed and the house was quiet, and the absence of my mother's excessive, bilious, Jewish portions of meat and vegetables, soon produced a dietary deficiency of which I was ignorant. My skin and hair changed, or rather deteriorated, and lost their healthy, shiny look, which I attributed to the fact that I was secretly anxious because of my underground habitat.

Those were the days of the first antisegregation marches, when in a moment of rare amity, the poor and middle-class joined to protest the mistreatment of Negroes in the South. It was a just cause and I felt that I should go and join the picket line.

One Saturday there was a march in the snow, in front of Woolworth's where I had bought my initiatory brassiere, and where you can buy anything provided it is quickly and cheaply made. Apparently their policies were like their items, they did whatever sold best, and forced the Negroes in the South to shop at separate stores.

So I put on my grey wool coat with its unnecessary Spanish ruff, leather gloves with a second wool pair underneath, a scarf, and high boots with wool socks inside, and then left my chamber with a token and self-righteousness in my pocket. I could smell my mother in what I was doing, and to this day whenever I do anything with a blind, heady sense of righteousness and purpose, the result is invariably catastrophic, particularly to me, which makes me feel that there is something in me profoundly opposed to philosophers, or at least to their systems.

When I got to the store, not only was it freezing, with the relentless, beating cold the New York City winter heaps on its inhabitants, but we had to keep moving in line, in a constant circle, as the police stood by with their hands in thick black leather gloves on their gun holsters and clubs. There was a clear threat in their attitude as they pushed or yelled at us if we stepped out of the circle. From the way one policeman in particular kept trying to arrest me, I decided that I must rouse some latent ire in these men; perhaps I reminded them of their young daughters who they could not control. I fought off the same policeman with the conviction that I was doing something "right."

There were Negro women with light children and white women with dark children, there were students dressed in dungarees and scarfs, whose presence suggested comfortable, bourgeois homes with plump, well-fed parents. There were skinny intellectuals and round housewives. Mixed in with a different, more violent expression, were poor workers in warm, dark clothing. This was a historic moment as everyone screamed and carried picket signs or hand-made posters, in which the implacable rivalry between the two classes dissolved before a common cause. One enormously fat white woman screamed relentlessly as she dragged her mulatto children, who were also crying, with her. It was the children's crying that penetrated most in the cold, indifferent streets. The noise swelled and echoed in my head like a drum. Then I realized that the pamphlet I was distributing explained nothing about why we were marching, and instead directed the confused or indifferent shopper to an incendiary rally two weeks in the future. I heard a drum beating somewhere as I stepped out of line to explain why we were there to people who stopped and asked me. This apparently was illegal, because each time I stepped out, the same policeman said, "Lady. If I catch you again, I'm going to take you in. You got to keep moving."

This continued for several hours. I left the line, he started to arrest me and I reluctantly went back into line. Soon my hands and feet were totally numb and I developed a strange, light feeling in my head. The noise and screaming boomed around me. The fat white woman with dark children was screaming and waving her thick fists into the air as I heard, "Lady, I warned you." Then I heard a drum beating again near-by and looked for it, thinking that somebody had brought it to attract more attention to us. When I could not find one, I realized that it was the beating in my own head, as something in me went back and forth, that I had mistaken for a drum. The beating increased. I turned around again to look for the drum behind me, and the next thing I knew I had a nightmare in which a black and white beast with a cap was trying to eat me up as it shook its fists, which were a woman's, in the air. I woke up with my head moving convulsively on something hard.

My mushrooms had apparently succeeded, and I had fainted and cracked my head on the cement street. I say apparently because I couldn't remember anything except the strange, light feeling, like down, in my head. So the doctor who clipped the hair from the bloody area on the back of my head told me, adding that I was anemic, but it was nothing to worry about. Then he turned me gently on my side, on a white examining table in the emergency room, and I felt the odd sensation of a needle going back and forth into me like cloth.

"Will I be all right?" I asked the handsome young intern. "I don't have much money."

"Oh sure," he said. "Just try to eat meat, and rest."

Then a familiar, partly bald, malevolent face appeared. "See what happens when you leave home," it said.

"Are you her father?" the kind, young intern asked. "She's a little undernourished."

"Yes. Are you coming back, now?" The same voice asked.

"No. I want to be free."

"You're still the same."

But I paid no attention to my father. Instead I thanked the handsome doctor and checked to see if the clipped area was visible underneath all my hair. It wasn't, and so I took the subway home, and crept back happily with my five stitches into my hole, from which I could soar freely even if I was anemic. That night, as I pulled the army blanket and feather quilt over me, I noticed that the furnace hadn't altered its sour expression which reminded me, for some reason, of my father, partly because the large door in front was like his moustache and partly because I was always afraid it would explode during the night. In addition, it was green like the old Plymouth we had when I was a little girl, which had also reminded me of my father's face because of the grill under the hood. I felt to see if the little red garnet Joseph had given me was still on my right hand. It was, and I was free, as my mind flew into its other world where it nestled like a bird, and I fell asleep.

20

When spring came between intermittent blasts of rain and even snow, and when the lengthening grey shadows formed perpendicular crosses of black on black in the alley between my habitat and the rose garden, as the light whitened and became increasingly clear, I thought more and more of leaving for California and Joseph went to the Bahamas to supervise the construction of several factories there.

One evening as Sara and Michael were eating their miserly, pinched portions of fleish mit kartoffel, and as Sara surveyed both me and the theoretical dirt with the same air of knowing disapprobation, although we stood in equal relation to the mathematical working of her household and in fact, hardly existed at all; while then, they were nourishing themselves with expressions that indicated heroic survivors of "over there" among which I was a potential element, I left them and went downstairs to my bedroom beside the boiler to pack my few things in a bamboo satchel.

"Turn out the light in the hallway," followed me in dangling tones which already shook with nerves and all sorts of menacing disorders as I reached the bottom and turned on the little light next to my bed. The boiler, as usual, peeped and gurgled and reminded me, like my father, of its implacable existence.

Then I took a bath and packed all my summer clothes to which suntan oil and sunglasses had now been added, and calculated that I had a few tokens for the subway and about twenty dollars. All of this went into a large, leather pocketbook together with a little black mascara. Then taking a last tour of the diminutive circumference of my netherworld hole, I surfaced with my satchel and pocketbook and the firm determination to tell them nothing.

Above, all was frugal peace and sanctimonious menagerie as Sara did the dishes and checked for hostile pieces of this or that and Michael put his glasses on and off his nose as he outlined his Swiss Alpines and chalets in black before he went in, trembling by inverse relationship to the innocent mountain target he was aiming for, in all directions and particularly from side-to-side. "Ach mench meier," I heard as the brush apparently missed. Apparently, I say, because with all the frills and unnecessary punctuation, it was impossible to tell where, exactly, the brush had hit. So Uncle Michael, with shaking determination and the resolve to let nothing hinder his jet-like advance toward his objective, took off his glasses which he required as part of a World War II wound and traced the circumference of the missed target with his moving nose. Then all was porcelain and happy comfort as he found the black dot, aimed for the spot and then brought down the brush, which wavered and quivered as if it were going to fall out of his hand altogether because of all the music, and he painted a rose blotch next to his nostril. Miraculously, the red went inside the black and even Uncle Michael's nose moved in happy accord with the patch which looked like a rose-garden beside a chalet.

As the two completed their sympathetic maneuvering, by means of which specks and blotches appeared and disappeared with culinary regularity, Aunt Sara took off her rubber gloves with her usual air of martyred cleanliness, as if the enemy had been stalled and closeted once more, and even Uncle Michael lifted his glasses from his one good eye in evident triumph at having placed his jolts successfully over the oil. During this momentary epiphany made of a nexus of noodles and screaming, I appeared in a rush from down below with my complicated gear.

Then was this antiseptic harmony and latent genius disrupted and smashed as Michael began to shake, trembling from some resiliant center of nervous disaccord, and Sara told

100

him to be careful or he'd have to go back to the doctor. He whirled his bad eye into his head where it landed and reverberated, and as he put his glasses down, he asked me in a suspicious tone where I thought I was going. Sara was a speedier judge and I was evidently already in her broom closet with Hitler and other determined personnel.

Then Uncle Michael gave up, since it was clear that I was leaving no matter what they did, and simply ignored me and went back to comparing his Alpine slopes to a small postcard. "Did you shut off the lights?" he asked from his brushes and noodle-like trembling as I was already in the front door. "The electricity bill . . ." The sanctimonious, Teutonic sequel to his formulaic question was lost as I heard my mother, eternal and malevolent, in his nasty looks and electric tone.

From the front steps I saw the two at their perpetual post, as if Rodin or some great sculptor had welded them into one avaricious mold. There they were. One form of twin parsimony, with their martyred heads close, to ward off by their artistic stasis, the recurrent enemy in the shape of me or costly life.

Several days later we walked arm in arm to the tropical rain forest at the top of a hill. Joseph wore his invariable silk, beige suit and I a good, brown linen dress. We went on, up from where we were high above the harbor, until the island and its inhabitants were lost in the fine, wet greeen curtain which we pushed aside as we entered. Inside the rain forest, the foliage peered and poked out of the tiniest crevices until it grew mathematically and became giant palms and ferns. Green became green as verdant braids of color hung down everywhere. Water trickled along slowly in a little stream until it collected and then fell in drops onto a natural stone basin. Underneath, the stream reformed and then continued on through the forest. There were bursts of purple blossoms and dangling palms and all sorts of moss and light stream algae. There was no end to the variety and ardent multiplicity of the entire mesh which covered the earth as a hymn to hot, animal life and procreation. Each element grew and entangled itself independently of its neighbor and the result was a green mixture in which the internal elements were in chaotic harmony with the outer mold. There was unending mathematics in this rain forest which obstructed the simple path the islanders had made to get from the capital to the outlying villages. It was as if nature, in despair at the proliferation of its own substance, had found a slide rule to multiply the inordinate number of its own, hot material.

Suddenly to the left of the spray under the yellow basin, a small boy with black bangs and black eyes crouched on his uncertain legs as he spun a pot on banana leaves. In spite of his primitive apparatus—he had only the banana leaves, clay and spray to work with—a perfectly balanced, even clay pot rose between his hands and was cooled by the steady stream. He had only a rag on his diminutive middle, but he looked up at us with one of the beautiful faces of the island's small children. When they are young, their tan skin and dark hair and eyes seem to come from some prior race which was closer to the sun. His expression too, was a mixture of the expectation of help and fear of an alien, invading race as he stopped spinning the pot and crouched on his toothpick knees.

As the pot remained motionless on the banana leaves and was cooled and tempered by the continual spray from the stone basin, the little boy turned his light profile to us so that the harmony of his young, tan features was in striking disproportion to his rickety bones and the negligent rag on his slightly protruding stomach. As he stayed in that position, torn between the wish to protect his pot, from which he and his family probably lived, and the equally strong wish for help, I saw that he was in fact, one of the hundreds of children who are magnificent until they grow up. The island's nutrition, however, is inadequate to sustain puberty and so they lose the needle and thread of their natures and soon look like beggars or poor workers.

He continued to stare at us, as children do when they are not sure what to expect, and his large eyes, like reversed moons, seemed to open even wider in either fear, or hunger, or both, like poor animals when they come to beg.

"Can I give him a quarter?" I asked.

"No," Joseph replied, angry at the question. "They are stealing all my valuable parts at the factory and all the sabotage is slowing us down by several months."

"But he's just a little boy."

"No," he repeated, as I sensed the basin-like contortions I could not see. "Let's go. We are pumping millions of dollars into their starving economy. Without us they would die altogether."

As I hurried to catch up with Joseph, I turned to see the boy still crouched under the basin beside the pot. He stared at us with eyes that opened increasingly in fear, either because they were looking into their own future or else for some other reason he did not understand. He was the first of many dark children I met when I traveled, for whom I always felt the same mixture of love for something beautiful and different and hopeless. Then the fear in his eyes became perpendicular to his fate, and the curtain of the forest closed over him and he disappeared.

When we were outside, the harbor formed a long, white semicircle between two layers of blue. It was made of grey and beige clusters of parched hills which dwindled off at the outer edge as they were worn away by the sea. The harbor looked like the cracked rim of a white porcelain plate and was neither beautiful nor ugly, but something antecedent. Apart from tiny bits of clouds, it was all white, impeccable hope and the dread of its opposite. Nothing living or sensate could penetrate the antique dryness of the place which seemed to increase and find its impetus from its own dessication. Joseph sat down on a boulder along the path, and I next to him. The little boy had obviously annoyed him by reminding him of all the pillage in his half-constructed factory and he wanted to be alone. Not all the harbors and rain forests in the world could stir him from his own interests.

"Just leave me alone for a while like a good girl," he said as he perched like an immaculate horus on the rock. There was no need to verify the tics and contortions and the battery of other, unwilling paraphernalia, although I could only see the fine line of his even profile. "What does she understand?" he thought to himself. "She worries about little children whereas I . . . I am attached to this thing." So as the diminutive circumference of his own little world began, sans hope and sans the expectation of anything other than itself, I left him alone and remembered, instead, a small clearing in a pine forest, many years before.

Our neighbors had placed their triumphant bellies, like beer cans, over their knees and everybody watched my father in one of the rare moments I had ever seen him happy. "Look, Cookie, they are doing it," he said. "Be careful not to knock the beer cans over or they will run away." As my father placed an acorn in each can and watched the chipmunks run up, grip the metal lids with their nervous paws and then bury their faces in the cans so that all you could see was their pretty tails, his face acquired a round, honey look in which the grinding misanthropy disappeared into some far-off, inaccessible place. "Hurry up, Susan," he yelled to my sister, "Come and see the chipmunks. They're starting to learn." As we three sat on the tree stumps which the campers had cut for their tents along the verdant arc of the wheeling, late spring afternoon, our paunchy neighbors watched and even my sister was momentarily devoid of worry or that indifferent matter into which Nature had dipped her unconscious soul. Then the buzzing chipmunks went in and out nervously of the cans until they became confident and forgot about us and just nibbled up the acorns which were falling everywhere. "It took time to get their trust, but I did it," my father said proudly, dressed in khaki work pants and a lumberjack shirt. Gone was hate and basement calculation. It was all chipmunks and beer and the thoughtless repose of the cool afternoon.

Then the neighbors opened more cans and I wished fervently that I would learn to like beer so I could get a belly and drink like a man. "Do you like them, Cookie?" my father asked as the incredibly pretty chipmunks flourished their tails like American flags in the small clearing in the forest near our tent. "Let's go," my father added as he displaced the cans in order to force the chipmunks to move.

"Let's go back," Joseph said when everything nervous had subsided into its opposite and resembled the sky above the

104

harbor. "I want to drive over to the plant before dinner to see how the foremen are doing." So I took his arm and we went silently back over the path until we got to the hotel. Below us the broken piece of porcelain stretched out, hot and immutable, as a testimony to alien, magnificent life and the opposite of what we were.

On the final evening, the sky looked like an old-fashioned bottle of blue perfume. It was heady with the collision and reformation of its own, warm elements. I have never seen such a sky again, except occasionally in Paris during the summer. We walked side-by-side to the end of the man-made reef which extended out into the harbor to ward off the barricuda and other carnivorous fish. Joseph wore his invariable beige, silk suit which hung at loose angles to his lean, tanned body and I, the same brown linen dress and black sandals.

As Joseph sat on the reef, while the sky above was full of hope and pendulous, fecund imagination, the fragile lever between us went all the way to his side as I remained motionless in the sand and waited for him to speak. Nature was all tacit charity and the myriad combinations of its dry elements as the lever continued to bang against its antipode and refused to move or acquire the momentum needed to generate a flicker. And so we remained in this bizarre position, as he stared into nothing, or at the sea, or into a hybrid kaleidoscope of his own construction. He resembled an ancient, mummified animal that perches, forever attentive and immobile, on a striated box within a tomb.

Then the lever flickered momentarily and the cryptic, painted animal showed some slight inclination for life and the return of its combative instinct. Joseph turned toward me so that I saw the weak side of his straight profile and said, lisping out sideways in his habitual manner with a muffled, New York City accent, "Well, Anne, here we are. Now do you see what you've done?" There was another pause. He turned away as the kaleidoscope shifted and resorted its problematic elements. Then the same material gathered a slight, incandescent hush which was nevertheless devoid of normal life and animus and he said, turning away, "I didn't want to love you. But you nagged and nagged and finally won."

There was no longer any truth to the truth and the cup of our lives had been emptied and returned to its former, morning position, but I nevertheless said, "I love you."

"Yeah." He turned away and then heaps, whole eons of whorehouses and machination leapt into this neon spot which had just been relighted and would now glow with independent life and subway doing. "Much good that will do tomorrow."

"I'll be back."

"So will Santa Claus. It's like I always told you, Anne, life is clean, honest work and intelligent fun. The rest is decoration."

Then the same dim material, at a loss for a direction or a target outside itself, turned inward so that it began to eat its own light and there was a proliferation of shade. From like to like, Joseph became more somber as there was a growing patchwork of incandescent pieces. Meanwhile, I never felt more confidence in my slender figure and ample scholarships and I thought of an old, Greek myth I had once heard. Apparently, there was once a king in the prime of life who, because of an ancient curse, would have to die unless he could find someone to take his place. So he searched everywhere. His children were too young and wanted to live; his parents too old and wanted to savor what was left to them of life, and in short, everyone found a good excuse to go on living. Finally, as he was about to sink to Hades, he asked his wife, who agreed and then died for him.

Similarly, I felt that if it were necessary, I would die for Joseph. But another, more clear voice told me that it was impossible to live for him and equally impossible to die for him and that from that night on, our lives were hopelessly separate and not all the myths and wishes in the world could change that one penny.

And so there is a bridge between men and women which momentarily binds them as if it were of the strongest steel. And while the core is made of multiple, metal threads which lie at parallel lines to the main artery, traffic flows and passes back and forth over the water. But if once that is disrupted, and the myriad cables cut or dislodged, then the same vehicles must find another route and can never again use the old, arithmetic path.

"You see," Joseph repeated, as he sat on the reef like a sphinx or horus or some other hidden, unfathomable animal that is neither living nor dead but in an in-between state that is hard to define. "It's like I always told you. Tomorrow I'll be left with my wife and psychiatrist."

Then I felt the arc of the tropical night and my tiny waist and the vast scope of the universe which reached above us in that alien, impoverished land like an eternal cup of hope and sweet solicitude. Meanwhile, a tear fell on Joseph's silk, beige pants, and left a small, wet stain. I thought to myself that you never know a man until you see him cry. Silently, effortlessly at last, the sad, little soldier climbed his problematic steps into the sky, as from time to time, a tear fell on the suit leaving a momentary spot which was soon dried by the dark, intrepid night.

21

Houses are like families. Once they begin to decay no one pays attention to the small things that go wrong until soon the whole building is about to collapse.

When I left Sara and Michael's at the end of the summer, my subterranean quarters were momentarily vacant but soon filled by my mother who moved into their brighter front parlor upstairs with its large windows which were hung with floor-length, white-lace curtains of the type that are only found in Europe. Although she fought continuously with Michael, there was a form of special entente or collateral misery, before the quarrelsome, tyrannical male, that bound Sara and my mother. The two were very much alike, with the difference that my mother had heard of the twentieth century and needed to identify constantly with the unhappy and underprivileged, whereas Sara only tended to her own pots, so to speak. In addition, there is a ghetto sympathy among Jews. They will hound you once you are inside, but they will not leave you on the streets or among strangers.

On one of the rare occasions when I visited my mother, we sat together on Sara and Michael's tidy sofa which was upholstered with a thick cloth which had a red and yellow design of roses and tulips. Beside us was a fine wood cabinet with a glass door that revealed costly silver and glass objects. There was an oval, hand-crocheted lace doily with intricate borders, carefully placed under glass, on the wood coffee table in front of us. With an increasingly trapped, suspicious look in her yellow-grey eyes, as her nose went up into the air as a sign of trenchant defiance, my mother said, as she sipped her coffee from the invariable white porcelain cup with its little, pink rose pattern, "Sheis! I told myself. If my daughter won't put up with that . . . that monster and moved out, why should I, the mother, stand it . . . that insensitive beast, ach, sheis . . . so many years of my life . . . so I came here. And let me tell you . . . Michael is not all there either. You understand me, but he took Sara out of Germany and, well he is old and has old-fashioned prejudices. He thinks women are . . . cooks and domestics like Sara, who does nothing but clean and listen to his complaints all the time, but I will have to get an apartment and alimony because he will not want to pay, but I will take him to court and fight. I have the right, after all those years of my life. Besides, what can I do to earn a living? Sell shoes, again, like my parents did in Germany and worry about whether they have flat feet, or straight feet, or corns or no corns. But let me tell you, Anne, the important thing is to keep on living, fighting. To struggle. Why? Aren't you listening? You think you know better than your mother, don't you? You never were an understanding child. Ach. Ja, ja. That's life. What can I do? Even my own children . . ." She sipped her coffee as her teeth, with their thick porcelain crowns, made a slight munching noise mixed with saliva, as they clacked against the cup's fragile, porcelain rim.

As for my father, it was during this period that he sat fully dressed in his grey workman's pants and red-and-black lumberjack shirt listening to the termites chewing away at the walls and foundations. He sat on the worn easy chair, which had declined to an indefinite, greenish-grey color and was placed between the kitchen and the large room with the old Knabe, for days on end without leaving the house.

He wore the old-fashioned gold watch with its pink face on his thick wrist through which the blood circulated slowly, as if against the will of the mechanism of which it was a part, and stared and worried about nothing for hours, as he subsisted entirely on bread and butter and coffee to which he added large portions of cream and sugar so that it was as sweet as cake. I sometimes thought that the rancid look in his eyes and colorless, unhealthy skin, came from all that sugar, or else that it went directly into the corners of his eyes to produce the unattractive, white mucous. Do you know how a small defect sometimes represents a person's soul to you? In this way, the mucous represented his slow, ugly deterioration, particularly since it lodged itself in his eyes.

At the time, however, I knew nothing about him or our old house and only wanted to go home and pack my things so I could leave for school in California. With this in mind, I knocked on the door of our house, one afternoon, and my father immediately let me in.

The moment I entered and saw my father slump back heavily on both arms into the green easy-chair on which he had been sitting, I knew I had made a terrible mistake. His neck was thick and turned sideways slowly, like the tin-can man, as if the screw to which it was attached was rusty and reluctant to move. He was fully dressed, although he was only keeping our house company. He must have counted the days by watching the thin black second hand on his watch go round until the large black needle struck off another hour.

There was the invariable speck of white mucous in the corners of his eyes, and his face had its usual expression of gloomy misanthropy to which a hungry, enclosed look had been added. The poor lost dog with its pretty, pathetic face, which is how he looked when I was a little girl, had become a wild, vicious animal.

As he glared at me, his eyes had a pinched expression, like someone who has been sitting in the dark for a long time and is unexpectedly exposed to light. Then without saying anything, as his eyes squinted either from the attempt to adjust to the light which was coming in from the front room or else because he had just been sleeping, he went to the windows and the front door and locked them all carefully. Then he took off his wrist watch and laid it on the bannister, which was also between the kitchen and the living room, while I tried frantically to think of how I could escape. I went through all the windows and doors in the house, including the basement, but there was no way I could get by him.

110

"Why did you come back?" he asked, hitching up his pants and adjusting his belt around his stomach, which stood out like a small ball. He had the expression of a murderer who needs to work up his anger and justify his wrath before he can actually slaughter his victim. There was one difference, however: I knew he needed me alive.

"I have to get my things," I said. "I got a scholarship to Berkeley and I need my old stuff."

"Scholarship. I'll teach you. Scholarship. It's all Hunter's fault. They made you a snob by putting all those high-falutin ideas into your head. I told you to get married like a normal person and cut out all this crap. You brat. Come here."

Then he adjusted his belt, although it was in no danger of falling off the rotundity which held it up, and looked around to make sure we were alone. Then he started to come toward me like a slow, slouching animal, with an indescribable . . . do you know the feeling that you are about to be murdered and that if you do anything at all to protect yourself, even the slightest movement or gesture, it will only hasten your destruction and so you must lie prone and mute until it is over and the murderer has finished with you. That precise moment, of expecting to be destroyed simply for existing and daring to breathe in my own particular way, together with the peculiar stiffening of the limbs that numbs them, has stayed with me and done me the most damage. And so I think it is the expectation of pain which is worst. Once the beating is actually over and done with you can lick your wounds and find solace in something or other.

"All right, you brat," I heard. "I'm going to fix you once and for all. I've had enough of your back talk."

Then, when I had given up hope and prepared myself by tightening my body from the neck down so that I would feel his hands less—it's impossible to flex the muscles in your face, which are too delicate, in the same way—and after I felt the flow of a horrendous "ahhh" in me, which also protected me from physical pain, just then there was a loud noise and a crash in our front yard. The iron front gate clanged shut and we could hear the noise of playing children.

"It's those damn kids again," my father said, "they're stealing

111

the roses." He left quickly to chase the neighbor's children from our yard and I took my chance. The minute he was gone, I ran out the hallway, through the front gate, and down the street where I had played as a child, crying uncontrollably.

Oh, yes. I did go back. At the candy store where I had bought macaroni salad as a child after school from the grotesquely fat woman who was still there reading a newspaper, I telephoned the police. Then warning the two who arrived that there would be serious damage if they left me alone with my father, I re-entered and packed my things.

I left our house a quarter-of-an-hour later with a policeman on either side and never returned.

In the official blue and white car, one tall policeman with his black cap on his head, turned to me and said, "Because you're a nice girl, we're going to take you to the subway. But it's against the rules and we could get in trouble. We're just supposed to drop them at the nearest bus stop or corner, but we'll make an exception this time."

Then the shorter, stout one who was driving, also with his cap on his head and who had an uncomfortable, unhappy look in his eyes of the type that usually finds expression in criticizing others said, looking at me through the rear-view mirror, "It's the Negroes who really mistreat their children. Just yesterday we found a little black boy, only four years old, drowned in the pond on the other side of town because no one was watching him. He just wandered off by himself and fell in. We had to drag the pond with a net and we finally fished him out, dead, like a sponge. Those Negroes just don't give a damn about their kids."

"Yes, yes," I thought to myself, holding my few possessions in my lap and continuing to cry uncontrollably, "Keep on. My father is proof that the Negroes mistreat their children." As I sat in the back of the police car that drove me away from my house forever, I had the vague, tenacious feeling that the whole thing was beginning again.

Now in the space where hatred and numbness should be and still are, I sometimes hear another voice, my father's, and I ask myself in what he could have found comfort during that time when he sat alone, fully dressed, listening to the termites eating away the walls and roof.

In my mind's ear in which I often hear the voices of those who are gone, I hear him saying, "Mother, why did you bear me? Knowing what life is, and you knew very well since you worked all the time and wound up in the poorhouse, why did you do it? I've worked hard for eighteen years, and nothing is left and the kids are gone, and the house is falling down. Listen, can you hear it? So, Mother, why was I born?"